THOSE
IMPOSSIBLE
ENGLISH

THOSE IMPOSSIBLE ENGLISH

BY

QUENTIN BELL

AND

HELMUT AND ALISON GERNSHEIM

GEORGE WEIDENFELD AND NICOLSON LTD
7 · CORK STREET · LONDON · W1

FIRST PUBLISHED
1952
IN GREAT BRITAIN
PRINTED AND BOUND BY C.W.S. PRINTING WORKS,
SOUTH REDDISH, STOCKPORT

CONTENTS

INTRODUCTION
by
QUENTIN BELL

I

NONE but the sternest adherents of that code which puts bread and butter before cake will read this essay before looking at the photographs to which it is, nominally, the introduction. Having seen those pages, the student of social history will not need, and others will hardly desire, more comment than is supplied beneath the pictures themselves. To go further, to attempt a connected historical narrative designed to illuminate these records of the past, is far beyond my powers. Nor do these pictures offer an adequate pretext for such an undertaking. Our exhibits have not been chosen at will; they represent a painfully selected fraction of the available material; but that material is, in its turn, strictly confined by the mechanical limitations of early photography.

The camera was still a toy of the rich and, almost, a novelty in 1850; it soon became the poor man's portraitist, but its scope remained very limited and it had to undergo a whole series of improvements before it could attain its present competent ubiquity. As we recede in time the sum and the variety of photographic evidence declines; a comprehensive photographic survey of the entire period is therefore impossible and, if it could be made, it would require not one, but many volumes.

Developments in the art of photography have produced a marked contrast between our earliest and our latest illustrations. The sitter of the Nineteenth Century is seldom taken unawares; he is given every chance to compose his features, to adopt a distinguished and agreeable attitude and to find his proper place amongst carefully chosen surroundings which subserve the general effect. The sitter of the present day may enjoy the same advantages and will, very probably, receive such discreet attention as may be supplied by the photographer's mystery. But in looking for our illustrations we have, for the most part, preferred those instantaneous and historically valuable indiscretions of which the modern camera is so often guilty.

In this it may appear that we have been unjust to our contemporaries. Nor can it be denied that there are some pages which lend support to this view. It may, for instance, be thought that Mr Sidney Stanley and his newspaper friends have been immortalised at an unflattering moment (No. 190). Perhaps it would have been kinder to have portrayed them before a painted backcloth representing the temple of Mercury staring, hand in waistcoat, at some appropriate ideal. The hero of the hour should have been in an exalted condition of conscious rectitude, while the gentlemen of the press, grave, reticent and censorious, withdrew to a becoming distance. In the same way the girl who shows us so much of her legs at a fun fair in Southend (No. 199) might have preferred some more dignified if less interesting pose. Here however, the advantages of the informal record become apparent, for here the sitter charms us by her unconsciousness of her own charm. The camera has fixed a moment of unreflecting agitation and delight which compares favourably with Miss Camille Clifford's preposterous effort to hold her breath and, at the same time, to look queenly (No. 120). Nor is there any more flattering picture in this book than that of two young women setting about their grim business of rescue amidst the shambles of Farringdon Market (No. 174).

No other form of art speaks with the impersonal authority of the camera; even when the picture has been artfully retouched the essential shapes of the subject remain insistently recognisable and will not be hidden. A photograph has much of the disagreeable candour of a mirror, and although there are few of us who do not clamour to be taken, there are fewer still who do not see in the result a libellous travesty. If we are ugly or ridiculous the sensitised plate will coldly inform us that this is the case; but if we are so unwise as to pose, or to make some foolish effort to impress that superbly indifferent apparatus, the final result will be still more distressing. The strained attitude, the rigid expression of false nobility or maudlin affectation, the flat painted backdrop, the unconvincing properties of the photographer's studio, the whole posturing absurdity of our feeble attempt to be impressive, is frozen and fixed for ever. There are some sitters and some photographers who can make these pretensions convincing; but the failures are much more abundant and they are entirely disastrous. Accidents of this kind are far more usual in photography than in the other visual arts because photography is an eminently accidental art. It shows (and this is its great merit) just how the sunlight fell upon the folds of a crinoline or the outlines of a workman's barrow at a given moment in history; and with facts of this kind the photographer must, broadly speaking, be content. In the work of Mrs Cameron, who was deeply influenced by the painters, the accidents of reality bring the spectator back to earth, even when the artist is being most violently poetic; for to some extent the photographer must stand back and allow Nature to speak for herself. The painter, on the other hand, must always be between us and his subject and must show us the Natural World entirely through his eyes. The example of Mrs Cameron's work which will be found in these pages is a little unfair and by no means her best work (No. 88); nevertheless it does serve to reinforce the argument; photography, because of its mechanical fidelity to Nature, is of supreme value to the historian; but it is a dangerous and unpromising medium for the expression of ideal conceptions.

Now the posed sitter in the photographer's studio is almost always attempting to conform with an ideal conception of himself, and that conception, inevitably, derives in large measure from the customs, standards, and aspirations of his age and class. Therefore we have in the Nineteenth Century portraits what may be described as a 'double exposure'. On the one hand the scientifically recorded image of the sitter as he now appears to us and, on the other hand, the deducible image of the sitter as he hoped to appear to himself. This desired image now stands at a double disadvantage for, not only does it usually fail to attain its original object; but, in that our social

2

aspirations are continually changing, it can at best conform to an ideal which we, on our side, can no longer accept. For example: take the Grecian beauty contest photographed by Jabez Hughes in the year 1882 (No. 89). Certainly it was inspired by exalted æsthetic ideals; and its failure to realise those ideals is due to the excellence of the photograph, which gives us an exact, and at times merciless description of character and appearance which, in a painting inspired by the same purpose, would have been generalised and sublimated. But, in addition to this incongruity, there is the fact that the intentions of those responsible for this remarkable picture are not easily appreciated or understood by a generation which no longer responds to the work of Alma Tadema and Lord Leighton.

The best companion to these photographs is therefore a study of the influence of social aspirations upon the habits, dress, ideas, furniture, æsthetics, and morals of our period; and particularly of that half century in which the recorded image is so much distorted by social principles which we no longer respect.

During the past hundred years England, like most other communities, contained a minority of rich people, a majority of poor and an intermediate class. Although the distance between the extremes has varied, together with the proportions and composition of all three groups, it is true to say that there has usually been quite an important minority which was in a position to purchase every convenience, delight and creature comfort that science and experience could devise. What should—but does not—astonish us, is the fact that these fortunate people could always have been more comfortable than they were, and that a great part of their wealth was spent in a manner calculated to produce neither pleasure nor profit. They were always ready to suffer boredom, discomfort and inconvenience comparable to that which the most backward savages undergo in deference to the taboos of their religion. A great part of this self denial and self mortification was indeed connected with religious observances; but much of the pain and discomfort, and nearly all of the seemingly pointless extravagance of 'good society', is devoutly observed without being divinely ordained.

The reader is probably familiar with the story of that king of Spain "who in great part was roasted, because there was not time for the Prime Minister to command the Lord Chamberlain to desire the Grand Gold Stick to order the first page in waiting to bid the chief of the flunkeys to request the Housemaid of Honour to bring up a pail of water to put His Majesty out".[1] The incident is probably imaginary but it is not so far from the truth as to be irrelevant, for it points clearly enough to the penalties of wealth and status. These self imposed pains become much more apparent when they are accepted by people who seek status without having wealth. Readers of Trollope will remember the principles on which the atrocious Mr Lopez regulated his unhappy household:

". . . he gave her to understand that he required from her very close economy. Then again she referred to the Brougham which she knew to be in readiness on her return to London; but he told her that he was the best judge of that. The economy

[1] Thackeray. *Book of Snobs*.

3

which he demanded was that comfortless heart-rending economy which nips the prac-tiser at every turn, but does not betray itself to the world at large. He would have her save out of her washerwoman and linendraper, and yet have a smart gown and go in a Brougham. He begrudged her postage stamps and stopped the subscription at Mudies, though he insisted on a front seat at the Dovercourt Church, paying half a guinea more for it than he would for a place at the side.''[1]

Compare this record of the 'seventies with the following observations of an American economist writing in nineteen thirty-four:

''Cars are selected not primarily for use, comfort or transportation, but to main-tain one's position in the community. The make, the model, the gadgets, the uphol-stery, are what counts. Many families have gone without milk for the children in order to buy gasoline for the car.''[2]

Here we are dealing with calculated sacrifices. In some cases, at all events, a materi-al advantage, such as an extension of credit or continuation in some genteel employ-ment, may be secured by social observances which, on any other count, must be classed as futile and even horrible. Here then let me add a modern instance of self mortification which appears, like that of the King of Spain, to have been undertaken in an almost religious spirit and to have benefited no one.

Some years ago I had frequent opportunities of meeting a lady who was consider-ably better looking and more fashionably dressed than most young women of the great city in which she lived. Her only displeasing feature was her left leg which, owing to some malformation, had to be supported by a hideous surgical apparatus. As may be supposed this defect compelled attention and made her, who would otherwise have been charming, an object of pity and of disgust. Now another eleven inches of skirt would have made the deformity invisible; but the prevailing fashion forbade such a skirt-length and the unwritten decree was meekly accepted. The case illustrates the tremendous force of custom and, in an extreme degree, represents a widespread hard-ship; for if deformed legs are happily few ugly legs are regrettably common and a uniform fashion in skirt lengths must either hide that which is beautiful or expose that which is not.

These sacrifices result from a serious and earnest desire to conform with whatever may be the prevailing habits of society and these habits are, in the last analysis, in-spired by the behaviour of the 'leaders of society'—the Leisure Class. The habits of that class were systematically investigated and discussed by the great American soci-ologist Thorstein Veblen in his book *The Theory of the Leisure Class*, which was pub-lished more than fifty years ago. I believe that Veblen's keen and irreverent vision is necessary if we are to have a clear view of social history: I must therefore devote a few paragraphs to a short adumbration of his central theory.

Briefly then: there is no class so class-conscious as the Leisure Class. Other strata of society are so busy accumulating wealth or attempting to keep alive that they have no time and small inclination in which to consider their uncomfortable positions

---

[1] *The Prime Minister.* [2] Stuart Chase. Introduction to Veblen's *Theory of the Leisure Class.* New York, 1934.

within the social pyramid; but those who sit near the apex of the structure think of little else and have abundant leisure in which to do so. Indeed their position depends upon a constant preoccupation with their own status and their whole lives are devoted to proving that they are what they are, that is to say, in economic terms, a class of social parasites. To this end they must—at whatever sacrifice of mere personal convenience—make it clear to all the world that they have all the characteristics of the true parasite. They must display their wealth by means of lavish and wholly unproductive expenditure; they must show in their education and their way of life that they rely upon the services of others and are entirely incapable of manual labour; their speech, clothes, manners, beliefs and occupations must be distinguished, noble and ornamental. (It will be understood that I am here describing the Leisure Class in its most perfect, and not in its actual condition.)

Veblen defines these methods of advertising status under the headings of Conspicuous Consumption and Conspicuous Leisure, to which he adds the very important and illuminating concept of Vicarious Consumption. His classification can best be illustrated by the history of dress; but since this has already been attempted we will here take another example, that of domestic service.

In the mid-Nineteenth Century the relationship between master and servant was very different from that which now exists between the employer of domestic labour and his employee. At that time the head of the household had the whip hand, the labour market was glutted and he could impose his (or her) own conditions. The slavey who sought a post had to submit to regulations which governed her private life, her hours and manner of worship and her dress. This state of things did not prevent the establishment of quite human relations between master and servant, but it implies something very like ownership. The suggestion of ownership made servants a useful means of proclaiming status. As an oriental prince was judged by the number of his concubines so was a Victorian householder judged by the size of his domestic staff. This, like his house and garden, his horse and his carriage, bore witness to his financial solidity, or rather, to his financial pretensions; for it was a common form of extravagance to keep more servants than one could strictly afford. This then is Conspicuous Consumption in its simplest, most ostentatious form. A more distinguished way of producing the same effect consisted in the employment of expensive servants, servants that is, who had received a long training, perhaps from boyhood (one of the conventional situations of comedy is that in which the servants of a parvenu are more at ease, socially, than their employer). The possession of 'old family servants' like that of old family silver, was something which all might envy and few enjoy.

Servants and wives are the chief agents of what Veblen calls 'Vicarious Consumption'. The amount that a single individual can consume in the way of victuals, comforts and dress is limited; for purposes of display it is therefore necessary to have an employee to consume on the employer's behalf and such a person ministers to the glory of his keeper. In this respect servants are rather like the guests at very large functions; they are present, not only to make themselves useful, but for a purely ornamental and uneconomic purpose, that is to say: to consume expensively and thus magnify the reputation of the man who pays. But whereas the guest is there to eat, the servant is there for show; he is above all things well dressed and in his eating, which is done in private, the principle of Vicarious Consumption will not apply.

The status of servants is clearly indicated by the use of expensive dress which, in modern society, is usually more elaborate and gaudy than that of the employer. A great man hardly has a more effective way of advertising his grandeur than that which consists in supporting a large army of leisurely and decorative flunkeys. And although there are, today, few private houses which can boast of more than a butler in evening dress or a maid in cap and apron, something of the old sumptuosity persists in shops, theatres, clubs and hotels. Theoretically, gentlefolk are incapable of any kind of menial labour and must therefore be looked after by domestics. Conspicuous Leisure is another aspect of Conspicuous Consumption and, in the Nineteenth Century, it was carried to surprising lengths. A Victorian gentleman might, and a Victorian lady would, expect the kind of attention which, nowadays, would only be undertaken in the service of an invalid. There were servants to ring bells and servants to answer them, servants to raise and to lower windows, servants to open and to shut doors, servants to drive the barouche and others to sit beside the driver and yet others to stand behind, there were servants to take the visitor's hat and coat, others to take his cane and his gloves, others again to announce him, there were servants to carve and to serve and others to fill the glasses—so that no bottle was seen upon the table until the servants had been sent away. Behind the scenes there were still more servants, cooking, dusting, blacking boots or fenders, making beds, washing dishes and beating carpets; while a separate race of helots looked after the gardens, the stables, the kennels and the gun room. In a great house the army of upper servants was so prodigious that a second line of under-servants waited upon the chief ministers of the Housekeeper's Room.

Of course things were very different in those suburban homes where the Browns enlisted the local grocer that he might wait at table and impress the Smiths.

Why the grocer? The answer is that the grocer was a man, and it was a typical feature of the whole system that men were employed wherever possible in the more ornamental duties. Women would have been quite as decorative and efficient, but women would have been more economical. 'That which is cheap must be nasty'; it is the first principle of Conspicuous Consumption. And it is the gross misuse and waste of manpower which lends opulent dignity to the service of butlers and footmen.

The liveried man servant is the perfect type of the vicarious consumer, and although he is dying out one can still find specimens; the days of his florescence are not far distant. But the pure consumer, the man whose entire existence is devoted to extravagant futility has for many years been extinct; he belongs to a social system which has been destroyed. These ideally useless creatures were rentiers, usually absentee landlords, completely ignorant of the process of exploitation upon which they depended and entirely undefiled by any connection with any sort of useful labour; not idle, but busily engaged in the otiose and absorbing flummery of a great court.

Aristocrats such as these no longer existed in the England of a hundred years ago, and in most other countries they were assailed from without and rotted from within; for the landowning rentier, if he develops at all, cannot avoid the creation of a rival who is not so nice in his habits. Thus, at a very early date, we find a class of traders, financiers and industrialists which, while affronting the power, apes the manners of the nobility.

The wealthy social intruder—the man who has made money by his wits but who wants to resemble those who were born rich—has been a stock figure of European Comedy since the time of Molière. The fun consists in his failure to achieve this end; but in point of fact great wealth usually prevails at last. Since the Reformation the mercantile classes of this country have invaded and to some extent have been assimilated by the aristocracy. The religious change deprived the nobility of a celibate profession for its surplus children, and it gave the noble houses collateral lines, which were employed in trade and in industry. At the same time political and social factors, such as the absence of a powerful monarch and the maintenance of an opposition party by a large section of the gentry, encouraged many landowners to live on, and eventually to develop their estates. The process was therefore one of interpenetration; while the oldest families in England were engaged in the exploitation of mineral rights, turnpikes, canals and horse-hoe husbandry; bankers, stock jobbers, and nabobs were purchasing boroughs, estates and titles of honour.

A concern for the more effective exploitation of the land was indeed recognised as a legitimate occupation of aristocracy. Rural development—which usually involved the bullying, cozening and liquidation of one's poorer neighbours—was too profitable a business to be neglected. The duties of a Justice of the Peace accorded naturally with these predatory activities; for enclosures, starvation wages and game preserving called for frequent exercise of the magistrate's powers. And so the rural magnates were very busy.

Nevertheless the aristocratic ideal persisted. 'Trade', as distinguished from the sale of agricultural produce and the collection of rents, was still considered base and ignominious in the mid-Nineteenth Century. It is recorded that the butler of one noble house threatened to go on strike rather than wait upon Mr Joseph Chamberlain (this can hardly have been before 1870). It was many years before the manufacturer of screws was accepted as being in all respects the equal of the holder of land, or of consols.

The reasons for this long interval between the political triumph of the commercial classes, which we may fairly date from 1832, and the final extinction of the belief in the particular virtues of agricultural exploitation, which can hardly be considered final before the reign of Edward VII, are to be found, partly in the modifications which the aristocratic ideal had undergone, and partly in the extremely thorough manner in which the mercantile classes emulated the gentry.

When Mr Marmaduke Muleygrubs had done well as a staymaker and ". . . had inherited a large fortune from a great dry salting uncle in Bermondsey . . . he cut the shop, and having been a rampant radical in the City, was rewarded with a J.P.-ship in the country." Cockolorum Hall, originally a farm house, then a villa, was transformed: "Massive stone towers, with loopholed battlements, guarded the corners—imitation guns peered through a heavy palisade along the top—while a stone porch, with massive black nailed folding doors stood out from the red walls of the centre. A richly emblazoned flag, containing the quarterings of many families, floated from the roof."[1]

This is fiction, but it is the fiction of a very accurate observer; compare it with the following extract from Hansard. Mr Labouchere is reported as follows: "Who were the gentlemen who were ordinarily made new peers? . . . He would take an instance, since it was one of the latest, that of Sir Henry Allsopp. . . This gentleman brewed beer, and by so doing acquired a fortune. . . . No doubt he voted very often for his party in the House of Commons, and very likely he subscribed to the Carlton Club. As a consequence he was made a baronet. No one objected to Sir Henry or anybody else being made a baronet. . . . But Sir Henry Allsopp was not satisfied with his Baronetcy and he was considered worthy of the dignity of a Peerage. This afforded good cause for complaint, for it gave him and his descendants the hereditary right of legislating for the country. . . . What was the first step that Sir Henry Allsopp took when he became a peer? He wrote to *The Times* complaining that he had been described as a brewer, and saying that he had ceased brewing; and at a bucolic festival which occurred in the county shortly afterwards, when his tenants congratulated him on being made a Peer, some gentlemen present suggested that Lord Hindlip (*né* Allsopp) was descended from the Plantaganet Kings."[2]

This process of intrusion and assimilation, which is closely allied to that emulatory process of imitation and aversion which we call 'fashion', implies admiration and acceptance of a particular way of life. That which is done in the 'best' circles will eventually be copied in the worst. There is an ideal to which all gentlemen or would-be gentlemen must strive to conform. It follows therefore that if we can gain a notion of what that ideal was we shall possess, not simply a picture of the manners of one class, but a prototype which informed the pretensions of every class that had any claim to gentility.

[1] See *Handley Cross*, by Robert Smith Surtees, Chapter xxxiv.   [2] Hansard, March 5th, 1886.

II

THE nature of the social history of England may, very roughly, be indicated by the development of one protean creature: the gentleman. Originally the word implied status and very little else. When Shakespeare makes Henry V say:

> "For he to-day that sheds his blood with me
> Shall be my brother; be he ne'er so vile,
> This day shall gentle his condition:"[1]

he almost seems to envisage a creation of gentry as extensive as that creation of peers which Mr Asquith threatened in 1911. The idea of gentle rank is even more clearly expressed in *Twelfth Night* when Olivia asks:

> "What is your parentage?"
> *Viola :* Above my fortunes, yet my state is well:
> I am a gentleman."[2]

Here the meaning is almost the same as 'noble'. We can measure the change between the 16th century and the 18th by comparing this purely hierarchical and amoral view of gentility with Burke's famous remark:

> "A king may make a nobleman, but he cannot make a gentleman."[3]

The confusion which these two conceptions of gentility have caused arises from the medieval habit of identifying moral qualities with social rank. Where the rank has disappeared the word has come to stand for moral qualities alone and such adjectives as: 'churlish' or 'villainous' do no more than remind us of forgotten prejudices; but in the case of the gentleman, the absence of a clearly defined rank and the pretensions of an exsurgent middle class have left the conception of moral excellence involved with that of wealth or social repute. When British colonists refer to the Malay as an 'innate gentleman' they mean, not only that he has many virtues and great charm, but that he is fond of sport and dislikes hard work. The word tends to broaden in accordance with the class structure of the nation; but it still contains a meaning which is social rather than moral.

When, therefore, we attempt to survey the life and habits of a gentleman in the middle of the last century we are at once confronted by a problem of definition. Our subject is not merely an aristocrat (though he need have no title) but a man of exemplary character although, as we shall see, he inclines rather to virtue than to rectitude. He was the cynosure and the palladium of the social order, and, just as 'economic man' exists most perfectly in text books, so the gentleman is most completely embodied in works of fiction. Perhaps he may be conveniently defined as 'that which most wealthy men aspired to be.'

He was expensive from the first. Numerous doctors, nurses and midwives assisted him into this world, where he was awaited by the best cradle and baby linen, the best nurse and nurse-maid, that money could buy. As his father's son he was an instrument

[1] *Henry V*. IV, iii, 61.   [2] *Twelfth Night*. I, v, 297.   [3] Letter to William Smith, January, 1795.

9

of Vicarious Consumption and, in consequence of this, he was more dressy at this early stage of his career than at any subsequent period. A cascade of ribbons, lace and frills contained the struggles and outpourings of early infancy. It was replaced by a fussy epicene garment and this, in its turn, was followed by what one can only call 'fancy dress'; for he was now disguised as a sailor, a soldier, a Highlander, or one of Van Dyck's lace and velvet infants (Nos. 44 and 45). Papa was a dark but glossy man, beginning in solid but lustrous boots and ending in a chimney-pot hat. It was not until he went to school that the infant paragon could imitate this sober and discreet attire.

He received an education suitable for one who was to occupy a high position in society. This limited the choice of establishments; there were not more than a dozen public schools to which his parents could possibly send him. The boy would be taught a great deal during the ten or eleven years of his preparatory and secondary education; but it was doubtful whether he would leave with more than a hundred lines of Horace and certain curious jingles—mnemonics concerning the gender of Latin substantives and the use of prepositions. Critics of the curriculum which produces learning such as this are invariably beside the point. The acquisition of useful knowledge, useful that is in a vulgar sense, is not aimed at or desired. No great harm is done if the pupil retains nothing save a marked distaste for the poets of Greece and Rome. The object is to furnish him with a number of classical tags sufficient to prove that a great part of his boyhood has, from a strictly economic point of view, been wasted; or, as they say, to give him the education of a gentleman. Of course there were always certain miserable swats who took their studies seriously, in the base hope of turning them to account and becoming dons—*docte sermones utriusque linguæ*; they might achieve their mercenary ends, but they could hardly avoid the contempt of their fellows.

This scheme of education was completed at one of our ancient universities (London already had a university but it was far from genteel.) These institutions fulfilled a two-fold purpose. They provided a certain number of dignified sinecures for the learned, and they formed a reasonably sheltered theatre for youthful experiments in the art of living. Here the student could prepare himself for the wider sphere of inactivities which awaited him in the great world. Here he received the elements of social training; he learnt what games to play, what wines to drink, what clothes to wear, what horses to back, what girls, and what wild animals to pursue. He was becoming a consumer in his own right. For a young man of means the process must have been sufficiently agreeable.

Home life, on the other hand, was decidedly slow. In that age parents demanded and exacted respect. It was an era which gave infinite opportunities for hypocrisy and pomposity and the father of the family was entitled, when it so pleased him, to be abominably rude to his children—even when they were quite grown up. Ladies, while suffering a great deal from the tedium of masculine talk, put an effective damper on those more adventurous topics, which formed so large an element in the polite conversation of former ages, and of our own. It is not surprising that young men of the upper classes sought the more congenial society of pimps, card-sharpers and thieves.

Volumes might, and indeed have been written, concerning the pleasures of gilded youth in that smug but violent epoch. Here it may be sufficient to disinter one of the forgotten scandals of the time; the story is unpleasant, but it is not uninstructive.

On September 19th, 1855, a performance was given at the Windsor Theatre for the benefit of one of the actresses—a Miss Conway. The lady was indebted for this favour, not only to Mr Nash, the lessee of the theatre, but to Lord Ernest Vane Tempest, a very young man holding a commission in a Guards regiment. Unfortunately for everyone concerned the youth was fickle and, while the performance was still in progress, he forced his way into the dressing room of another actress—a Miss Stewart —and insisted that she should have supper with him after the performance. When Miss Stewart would have none of him he refused to leave her dressing room. He kicked a dresser on the shins. He hit someone else in the face. He turned off the gas. These proceedings held up the performance on the stage and brought Mr. Nash upon the scene. Mr Nash, whom I imagine to have been a weedy ineffectual person, begged the intruder to leave and was told—amongst other things—to go to Hell. He then asked one of Lord Ernest's fellow officers to help (a great many soldiers appear to have been behind the scenes that evening). This officer laughed and said: "Get him out yourself." Meanwhile the house was in an uproar.

Mr Nash then sent for the police. When the constable arrived several soldiers called out: "Don't touch him. He's Lord Ernest Vane Tempest." This advice was very properly ignored; the intruder was expelled without trouble, and the incident seemed to have been closed. In fact, it had hardly begun.

Half an hour later Lord Ernest set upon Mr Nash, broke a stick across his back and dragged him to the top of a steep flight of stairs. "Now, you devil," he said, "You dared to give me in charge to a policeman; I will break your infernal neck."

"Do not kill me in cold blood," wailed Mr Nash; but his assailant was merciless; he flung the wretched man down the stairs and would have broken his neck—had it not been for the ready intervention of a scene shifter. Baulked of murder Lord Ernest followed his man down and began to pummel his face until, at last, his brother officers intervened.

Mr Nash went to the magistrates; he was angry, and with reason; but he soon found that it was not easy for a poor man to have the law of a well-connected officer. The justices tried to persuade him to compound with Lord Ernest and, when they found that they could not keep the matter out of court, they let the culprit go with a fine of five pounds. The military authorities, who might well have cashiered the young man for conduct which scarcely became an officer and a gentleman, contented themselves with sending him to the Crimea.

Mr Nash then wrote to *The Times*. *The Times* responded with a very strong leader which must have made unpleasant reading for the Windsor magistrates and for Lord Hardinge, who was Lord Ernest's uncle by marriage and was in command at the

B

Horse Guards. (*The Times* was at odds with that department.) In the correspondence which followed the magistrates got the worst of it and the editor had a great deal more to say about the War Office. But Mr Nash was less fortunate. He brought an action for trespass which came before Lord Campbell in December, 1855; the defendants family engaged the services of the Attorney General and, one suspects, of several of the plaintiff's witnesses. Mr Nash was made to appear, and probably was, an habitual drunkard who managed his theatre in so irregular a fashion that the offence—in so far as trespass was concerned—appears to have made but little difference to the customary disorder of his arrangements. A grand jury gave him twenty-five pounds damages and *The Times* forgot its indignation.[1]

Reading contemporary accounts of the affair one is struck, not only by the brutality and arrogance of the offender and by the very partial justice of the magistrates, but by the dreary squalor amidst which these provincial gaieties were staged.

From the stews, the cockpits, the caves of harmony and the gambling hells, the young man of fortune was eventually recalled to marriage and a career. The radiant and virtuous imbecile whom he married deserves all our attention and she is examined at some length below; in this place I want to glance at some of the occupations that were open to her husband.

The noblest employment of an eldest son was the government of the nation. In this service he might, eventually, gain substantial rewards; but the House of Commons was no place for a poor man. There was no salary and although, after the Reform Act, it was not so easy to purchase a borough outright, still, the process of getting oneself elected was very expensive; in fact the 'running expenses' of a member of the lower chamber were much greater than those of a peer.

If the young man preferred the administrative side of government he would almost certainly enter the Foreign Office. Here, the importance of Conspicuous Consumption and Conspicuous Leisure has always been understood. The functions of a diplomat, involved as they are with the life of courts, the minutiæ of protocol and almost unlimited opportunities for futile expenditure, have always made the employment legitimate for people of rank. There was, in those days, no nonsense about examinations; and the Courts of Europe, which were numerous before 1870, provided a great many sinecures for the decorative younger sons of our great families.

Equally far removed from economic utility, and equally genteel, was the Church. By this, of course, is meant the Established Church, for although there were a few dissenting peers and a great many plebeian anglicans, the Church of England was, to a large extent, the creature and the ally of the landed gentry. She was tied to the interests of that class, which held a great number of advowsons and was, until the Reform Act, the final arbiter of her doctrines and ceremonies. This fact is so momentous in the history of our country that we may pause to consider some of its effects.

[1]See *The Times* for October, November and December, 1855.

INTRODUCTION

The galaxy of English sects forms a pattern which, in large measure, corresponds to the class structure of the nation. The parson was assisted by the squire and the squire's immediate inferiors, the minister was supported by tradesmen and shop-keepers, the Wesleyans converted, and gained the allegiance, of the industrial masses. Thus, very roughly speaking, each class was provided with its own brand of religious belief.

Now this state of affairs has undoubtedly been of great service to the cause of toleration. The bitterness and violence which usually arises when Christianity is taken seriously by its supporters or by its opponents, has been progressively re-strained in this country by the sedative and moderating influence of party politics. For, while the theologians deal in rigid absolutes, the politicians must compromise and compound. In a country which contained a good many Romanists and a great many Puritans, party politicians have usually found it expedient not to take their own religious convictions too seriously. The disasters of Cromwell and of James II remained as valuable object lessons.

Religious hatreds die hard, much harder than those of nations or of parties. A young High Churchman of the mid-Nineteenth Century would probably have joined in the desperate efforts which were made to oust poor Mr Gorham from his living (he had the temerity to assert that Divine Grace might be accorded before Baptism and was supported in this view by the judicial committee of the Privy Council); he would have joined with equal vigour in the absurd hullabaloo that was made about the Roman creation of English Bishoprics; and he would probably have helped to delay the education act of 1870 and the admission of dissenters to the Universities. Nevertheless in all these matters the violent and deeply felt convictions of the ortho-dox could do no more than delay the imposition of a liberal solution. In public life it was impossible not to remember that, although the heretics and schismatics had souls to be chastened, they also had votes to be won.

The existence of a great variety of religions, all of them more or less in alliance with the political parties, had a decisive effect upon our political thought and temper in that great crisis of faith which affected the whole civilised world, and which may be said to have begun in the 'fifties and to have continued throughout the century. In those years the discoveries of the geologists, the biologists, the textual critics and the anthropologists worried our forefathers quite as much as any of our own hideous problems worry us. On the continent, and especially in those countries where the Roman Church had succeeded in stamping out all opposition, the liberal movements developed in opposition to the Church, and hence to all religion; in these countries therefore, scientific scepticism was a political weapon and was used by the anti-clerical movements. These derived from the Encyclopædists of the Eighteenth Century, and developed into the materialist socialism which, in our own time, has conquered one half of Europe. But in England, where no party had a monopoly of religion, liberalism marched under a non-conformist banner in opposition, not to Christianity, but to episcopacy. It was impossible, therefore, that any faction should profit by the advance of scientific materialism. The Churches fell back from one ill-prepared position to another; but they did so without losing their original formation. All alike were opposed to this new menace and no one stood to gain by their discomfiture. These peculiar conditions have given us a political climate quite unlike that of our European neighbours. We have gradually become extremely irreligious; but our scepticism is tolerant, for it has remained untouched by the enthusiasm of foreign atheism and foreign clericalism.

The Church and diplomacy were genteel professions; partly because they were traditional preserves of the upper classes and partly because, in the nature of things, they were far removed from any suggestion of menial toil. The same may be said of the armed forces; but in this case there is an even greater degree of merit, for the warrior is not simply unproductive; he is positively destructive.

The military man is held in honour, not only for his courage—the miner, the physician, the missionary and the mariner are as brave as he—but because he is a Conspicuous Consumer. His life is divided between Conspicuous Leisure and Conspicuous Waste. Despite its seniority, and the fact that it was at this time in the hands of a few well-placed families, our Navy was never quite as fashionable as our Army. For one thing it has never been quite as useless, for another it provides less opportunities for the display of wealth; it is difficult to combine the pleasures of the London Season with the duties of a fleet which must patrol the seas. Moreover, ships have to be treated in a more or less serious spirit and conducted with science, for they must remain afloat. The advantages of the Navy may be apparent in time of war; but in time of peace the army is a vastly superior vehicle for social display.

The army on the eve of the Crimean War was indeed a perfect medium for ostentation. The young nobleman who had purchased a commission in a fashionable regiment was not usually bothered by any tedious study of military science; he was expected to wear a handsome uniform, to know what orders to give on the parade ground, to amuse himself expensively, and to behave gallantly upon the battlefield. The army in which he held his commission rested complacently upon laurels which had been won by an earlier generation; this occupation had permitted it to develop from a war machine into a military ornament.

When war broke out the generals attempted to rehearse the half forgotten tactics of the Peninsular Campaigns, but in fact the conflict was undertaken in a spirit which suggests still earlier wars. The nation as a whole was not involved; the troops left amidst scenes of giddy enthusiasm; but it was taken for granted that the fighting would be left to them, and to them alone. There were so few patriots willing to freeze to death before Sebastopol that the government was obliged to recruit a foreign legion. This was war as the Leisure Class understood and enjoyed it. The representatives of that class were ready, as always, to act with reckless courage and, in some cases, to show great powers of initiative and improvisation; but it was still the era of decorative heroism, in which the officers of the opposing sides treated each other with elaborate courtesy, while the common soldier was expendable.

That the whole attitude of the military (in the higher ranks) to the comforts of the ordinary soldier was out of date, is shown by the sudden outcry of the press and public opinion at home when the horrors of the campaign were reported. The sufferings of the troops were no greater than those which British soldiers had undergone in many previous campaigns[1] and no one had ever bothered about such things in those days. The new element in the situation was not the callous incompetence of the War Office, but the humane conscience of the Nation. The general outcry of the public and the insistent interference of a frightened government, caused bewilderment and indignation amongst the aged generals and bureaucrats, who had for so long been in control. They were taken unawares as cannibals might be who, by some oversight, found themselves involved in the proceedings of a vegetarian summer school.

When the war was over the military authorities could return to the pleasing duties of soldiering. The lessons of the Crimea, like those of 1870 and the far graver warnings of the American Civil War, were forgotten or disregarded. The British Army fought many victorious campaigns against savage enemies, often in difficult country; but it never forgot that it existed primarily for purposes of display. In 1884 a young officer in Malta was fined by his mess for taking an interest in his profession (he had been so imprudent as to mention the Peninsular War).[2] The crime was serious, for it implied a belief that the army had occupations other than those involved in playing polo and arranging Gymkhanas. Those military exercises, upon which an exigent taxpayer insisted, were so devised as to suggest the minimum of professional earnestness. Elaborate and beautiful choreographic displays were staged upon the barrack square. Dense masses learnt to evolve in accordance with the principles of Frederick the Great. The British square, although it was broken by ill-armed savages in the Soudan, continued to be cultivated for its beauty until late in the century. Sir Ian Hamilton scandalised his superiors by entertaining the subversive notion that a rifle is an instrument for casting bullets at the enemy and not, as all right minded persons agreed, a stage property for the gorgeous rites of the parade ground.

In October, 1899, this magnificently decorative army was confronted by a force equipped with modern weapons and possessed by a prosaic and plebeian notion of warfare. Not unnaturally the more beautiful of the adversaries suffered a series of grave reverses and was obliged to learn rather more effective tactics on the battlefield. The nation was profoundly shocked and the generals returned from South Africa much sadder and a little wiser. Two World Wars were needed to complete the educative process; but undoubtedly the view that the army should not be purely ornamental, and should be made capable of meeting a well armed foe, became more and more widely held after the Boer War and, as a vehicle for the display of Conspicuous Leisure, the service declined from thence onwards.

[1] Sir John Fortescue in *Early Victorian England*, 1830-1860. Humphrey Milford, 1934.
[2] Dunsterville. *Stalky's Reminiscences.*

15

If an elder son were to do anything, then he could hardly go outside the Church, the Army, Diplomacy and Politics; there were however a certain number of dignified occupations in which a younger son might find employment without disgrace; these were: the other branches of government service, the Law (in most of its branches) and the learned professions. Certain activities which were profitable, and even useful, were open to a man of birth and breeding on the strict understanding that he treated them in a noble and disinterested spirit. A Cavendish or a Cecil might investigate the physical properties of matter without being suspected of any desire to make a profit. The study of living organisms has been less patronised by the nobility and gentry, perhaps because biological research is never far removed from the business of the apothecary. Pure Science, that is to say science which is *ostensibly* of no practical service to mankind, is clearly more genteel than those impure sciences which cannot be divorced from economic or biological necessities. Science, it was felt, should be the useless toy of curious philosophers.

The arts, no less than the sciences, offered a permissible occupation for the dilettante. It has always been possible for a gentleman to address the world through the medium of a publisher and even to pocket the proceeds of the undertaking. Literature, though a laborious, is not a menial task. (Journalism, being a whole time hand-to-mouth sort of business is ever so much less respectable.) But the other arts were different. In the Nineteenth Century the middle classes furnished the great majority of painters and sculptors and where, in former times, a few adventurers of genius had achieved comparative respectability, the rentiers now provided most of the talent and all the enlightened patronage. But it was still the less exalted classes which produced the artists. The aristocracy produced writers, but it produced no painters and, in the 'fifties, there was still something of the apprentice-trained mechanic about such artists.

Consider the case of the Lord of Burleigh. It will be remembered that when he addressed himself to a young woman of very humble origin he adopted a necessitous and ignoble disguise:

> "He is but a landscape painter
> And a village maiden she."

On these more or less equal terms they were married. As a mere painter he apologised for being able to offer her nothing better than that state of life to which she was accustomed. When the young bride discovered that, so far from being a landscape painter, he was a gentleman of good family in easy circumstances, the shock to her social feelings was so great that she went into a decline and soon died.

It was much the same with music; so long as he preserved his amateur status, a well brought up young man might indulge in this eminently social art (witness the illustration No. 22). Nevertheless there were censors who considered that there should be very definite limits even to such activities as these. "Gentlemen also sang", writes a trustworthy historian, "but play the piano gentlemen did not, that being considered a task only fit for ladies and professional musicians.'' [1]Presumably it was taken for granted that a lady could not possibly be a professional.

If a gentleman needs violent exercise he must seek it either in warfare or in sport. These are the traditional outlets for a nobleman's energy; for here he can be reasonably sure that his labours will be unprofitable and his expenses heavy. I suppose that, at the beginning of the Nineteenth Century, a country gentleman could undertake no grander extravagance than that involved in hunting his own pack of hounds; it must have been an enormously expensive proceeding. But to hunt two days a week with a subscription pack was, and is, a considerable undertaking and enough to mark a man's social status for, besides the horse (or horses) there was the pink coat and all that went with it, a great many tips and a mass of incidental expenses. A certain number of farmers might ride to hounds with their betters, but the majority of the field was certainly representative of the Leisure Class.

In the 'fifties and 'sixties hunting found a serious rival in shooting. Until that time shooting had been an expensive, but comparatively ill-organised affair; it lacked the social graces of the hunting field. The guns walked up to their game; parties were small, and there were only a few servants to load, carry the bag and manage the dogs. The invention of the *battue* changed everything. Now, great numbers of birds were reared like poultry until the 1st of October, when they were driven over the waiting ranks of sportsmen by an army of keepers, beaters and stops. The new method met with some opposition at the outset; but it soon became universal, for it gave an opportunity for spectacular shooting, prodigious bags, sumptuous al-fresco collations, and all the apparatus of expensive venery. But even this reckless prodigality was surpassed by the makers and users of deer-forests, who depopulated and made wasteful large areas of the Highlands.

Blood sports, because they form a part of the aristocratic way of life, have for centuries been highly organised; but games with a ball, although they have had their part in the life of courts, are less expensive and less distinguished. A ball game involving the use of expensive ponies was brought from India during the last century and has given us, in polo, the one thoroughly aristocratic game of its kind; but the emergence of a new urban class created the need for a new form of exercise sufficiently cheap to be popular and sufficiently futile to be reputable. Cricket and football were developed and recodified, croquet was invented, tennis adapted, golf was imported from Scotland. An enormous and ever increasing amount of time and energy was devoted to these pursuits. The middle classes expended their surplus energy on golf courses, while the working classes found in the spectacle of great contests a sure diversion for their leisure.

In nothing has the 'British Way of Life' been more successfully diffused over the globe than in this new and curious passion for propelling a ball hither and thither, or for watching others do so. Countries which have found our parliamentary system

[1]'Homes and Habits' by Mrs. Peel in *Early Victorian England*, 1830-1860, edited by G. M. Young. Mrs. Peel probably refers to a rather earlier period than that in which our photograph was taken.

unworkable have learnt to imitate and to surpass our athletes, nations which have thrown off the imperial rule still acknowledge the metropolitan status of Lords or of Wimbledon.

The distinction which we have already noted in the arts and sciences holds good for sport. It is thought nobler to kill deer than to destroy vermin, and a very sharp distinction is made between those gentlemen who play for the sake of Conspicuous Consumption and the 'player' who plays for money. Severe juries are appointed to make sure by their constant vigilance that those who claim amateur status shall never, for one instant, succumb to the temptation of profiting by their skill. And although the professional must usually play a better game than the amateur—and is not really a less moral person—it is felt that a pure and chaste glory attaches to the sportsman who is quite clearly and unequivocally wasting his time.

It must be said that during the past hundred years a great many members of the English upper classes have given their lives to useful ends. Some have devoted themselves to agriculture or to industry, others to religion or to politics. In fact the governing classes of this country have shown more sense of private enterprise and public duty than those of most other lands. One could find many examples of Englishmen who have used their fortunate station in life to further what they considered to be the good of humanity at large. And yet, how many obscure but expensive lives have been spent in a decorous round of futilities? Such lives have not been without their pleasures; ostentatiously or furtively a gentleman of the last century could gratify all his desires, nor was it wholly disagreeable to spend large sums in destroying one kind of animal in winter and even larger sums in wagering on another kind of animal in summer; even the ceremonies of a hopelessly tedious and philistine society may have had their compensations; but what enormous wealth and what tedious efforts were spent in making these simple pleasures socially reputable. Throughout his life the man of wealth was tied by the necessity of keeping up appearances, and when at last he caught a fashionable complaint and passed through the hands of a titled physician to the grave, he died extravagantly and was expensively buried.

III

THE foregoing brief but discursive remarks on the occupations of a gentleman were prefaced by an attempt to identify the subject of our enquiries. It is rather easier to determine the nature of a lady; for the title had not, and perhaps still has not undergone so complete a transformation. The notion of status, as opposed to that of moral excellence has, to a much greater extent, been retained. Nowadays the expression 'a great gentleman' can hardly be used without conveying a notion of moral worth; but a 'great lady' is recognised by her manners rather than by her principles; one does not infer that she is a good woman. In the same way it is much more usual to hear people talk about 'nature's gentlemen' than about 'nature's ladies', and although ladies may be coupled with gentlemen in ordinary parlance, a 'lady' is also the feminine equivalent of a lord. Women in fact would appear to be rather more genteel than men. They are the special objects of courtesy and their social potentialities are greater. When the upper classes began to ally themselves with rich American families and, later on, with the stars of variety, it was their sons, not their daughters, who made these interesting experiments in exogamy. It is widely felt that a woman of no family can acquire almost any status by marriage while men are far less easily ennobled. The law expresses this view in that it gives a woman her husband's title while allowing her to keep her own rank even when she marries beneath it.

These advantages may, at first sight, seem inconsistent with a system of law and custom which, until very recently, cheated and penalised women in almost every other matter; but they are not so in reality.

Society favours women in most questions of status and decorum because they are, or were, more useless and more ornamental than men. The completely ornamental man was at the very apex of the social pyramid; whereas women were, or could pretend to be, purely ornamental within a wide range of income groups. Women of quite humble families lived lives as conspicuously wasteful as those of the greatest peers. The wife or daughter of a manufacturer could be perfectly decorative; she was hardly affected by the industry of her men and the social repute of the family was, to a very large extent, in her hands. It was she who chose the curtains and made polite conversation with the vicar, it was she, and not her husband, who proved the family's capacity for fashionable extravagance by wearing a large number of expensive clothes. Given taste and intelligence she was as well equipped, and as free to consume on behalf of her husband, as were her social superiors.

As industrial society developed, the privileges and the disabilities of women became more important. While the improving landlord was unable to be wholly idle and the captain of industry could not be idle at all, the exemption of ladies from all forms of labour but one, became ever more essential to the status of the family. The dress of the sexes developed on ever more divergent lines, the taboos governing the relationships between men and women were strengthened, and the charms of feminine ignorance and stupidity were exalted.

So long as a woman did not actually do her own housework (servants were dirt cheap) she was free to magnify the social status of the family by a calculated regimen of costly indolence. Her life contained nothing more useful than a certain amount of Sunday School teaching and charitable patronage, nothing more vigorous than dancing or riding. Cards, gossip and various other social diversions, which might possibly include a political or artistic hobby, filled the rest of her time. If we consider the rich and pretty bondage of feminine dress between the years 1850 and 1900 it is difficult to see how any greater exertions could be undertaken. The illustrations which follow will be sufficient to indicate the cumbrous bulk of the earlier period and the crippling pressures of that which followed it. In fact there were women who could triumph over these impediments; but, ostensibly, they marked the wearer as a lady of leisure. It must however be remembered that it was only in the aristocracy and the higher levels of the middle class that women were exempted from the care and the elementary education of their enormous families.

The girl who was devoted to this domestic and decorative existence received an education which was, in some respects, less useless than that of her brothers; for he was made into a scholar and a gentleman, and for this purpose trained to learn that which could be of no service to anyone but himself; she, on the other hand, was intended to become a pleasing imbecile—as such it was proper that she should be taught to make herself agreeable. Whether she did this by ruining De Wint paper, misusing the pianoforte, arranging berlin wool and decorating family albums may be questioned; but there was a definite notion that these proceedings would enable her to obtain a husband.

Probably the underlying idea of those responsible for female education was similar to that of those who governed our great public schools. A girl might learn to play the piano or to speak French because, after all, there was no likelihood that she would be able to become a professional pianist or to use her linguistic knowledge in business. In her case all that mattered was that she should be spared any knowledge of housework or cookery. Her husband would be satisfied so long as he was certain that she knew nothing of these arts; the ladylike accomplishments, like his own classical tags, were evidence of her wasted education.[1] It is significant that the parents of other countries, in which girls were confined in convents, and in which a bride was disposed of as though she had been a pig in a poke, gave their daughters an education which was in most ways similar to that of our own freer system. Under both systems these accomplishments were usually abandoned after marriage.

Although the atrocious legal position of women could result in the infliction of very serious injustices, it may be doubted whether women of the wealthiest classes

[1] "Clara, Flora and Harriet were very pretty and very highly educated—that is to say: they could do everything that is useless—play, draw, sing, dance, make wax flowers, bead stands, do decorative gilding, and crochet work; but as to knowing how many ounces there are in a pound of tea . . . they were utterly, entirely and most elegantly ignorant." *Ask Mamma*, by Surtees. Ch. xxv.

suffered very severely under the laws and customs of a hundred years ago. Unless she were very unfortunate or very indiscreet a great lady had little to complain of save the intense boredom of her life.

"Our social restrictions were often irksome" writes one lady who was born into a fortunate home about eighty years ago, "but what I remember as much more so was the want of liberty in everyday life. How many a long dull summer afternoon have I passed indoors because there was no room for me in the family carriage and no ladies' maid who had time to walk out with me. We lived near St. James's and all the clubs, so that for my sisters or for me to go out alone in the streets would have been to defy the social taboo in its severest form."[1]

The theory, it seems, was that a solitary young lady would have been at the mercy of hordes of ravishing club-men. Things were better in Belgravia where "the men were chaste and the women were brave."

Real hardships were experienced by the daughters of those families rich enough to give their daughters a useless education, but too poor to give them anything else. In a society which contained more women than men and in which the sons of the middle classes were able to find employment overseas, the plight of an unattractive and undowered girl was damnable. Every profession in which a woman could use her brains or her hands was shut against her either by law, or by a fierce convention. Her only hope was to become a governess (under the circumstances it is not surprising that the profession was overcrowded and the wages miserable). Her life was then devoted to the task of instructing another generation of unfortunate young women in her own genteel uselessness. As a poor old maid she became the legitimate butt of youth, and she ended a hard and barren life without any security beyond the good will of her employers or relations.

The miseries and waste of this system were sufficiently shocking to provoke a demand for female education amongst intelligent women and fair minded men, and when once the possibilities of education had been canvassed, the demand for other employments arose and this was followed by an extended and sometimes violent demand for the suffrage.

The demand for education was gradually conceded and, in the seventies, women gained a precarious foothold at Oxford and Cambridge (No. 113). But the struggle for education was as nothing compared to the struggle for employment and the vote. Despite the fact that the only considerable leader of Englishmen in the Crimean War was a lady, the view that women should stay at home remained unshaken. The pretensions of the advocates of women's rights were dismissed with derisive laughter. The ladies were told that they were not to meddle with things which they could not understand. When those women who had managed to creep into the schools defeated the men in examinations, the laughter turned to fury; and steps were immediately taken to keep those impudent hussies out of professions, in which they showed such unwomanly ability.

[1]Lady Lovelace in *Fifty Years*. Thornton Butterworth, 1932.

Antifeminist sentiment in the professions often took a cowardly and despicable form; the doctors, in particular, showed by their violence that they were desperately frightened of feminine efficiency. But, in the main, antifeminism was a genuinely idealistic emotion based on a profound conviction regarding the economic role of ladies in society. A real horror was felt at the idea of a well bred young woman doing anything useful. There was a real belief that ladies were ornamental breeding machines, too stupid and too feeble to enter those professions in which men earned a living. The extent to which this belief was held may be judged from a public protest against any proposal to grant female suffrage, which was published by the *Nineteenth Century* in June, 1889. The Manifesto was drawn up and signed by ladies; amongst the signatories we find Lady Randolph Churchill, Mrs H. H. Asquith, Mrs Humphrey Ward and, most surprisingly, Miss Beatrice Potter (she changed her views before becoming Mrs Sidney Webb).

"To men", wrote these ladies, "belongs the struggle of debate and legislation in Parliament; the hard exhausting labour implied in the administration of the national resources and powers . . . all the heavy, laborious, fundamental industries of the state, such as those of mines metals and railways . . . In all these spheres women's direct participation is made impossible either by the disabilities of sex, or by strong formations of custom and habit resting ultimately on physical difference, against which it is useless to contend . . .

"We believe that the emancipating process has now reached the limits fixed by the physical constitution of women, and by the fundamental differences which must always exist between their main occupations and those of men."

Now the signatories must have been well aware that women were capable of 'hard exhausting labour' far exceeding that involved in a parliamentary contest.

"Females" says a report published forty-seven years earlier, "submit to work in places where no man or lad could be got to labour in; they work in the bad roads (of the mines) up to their knees in water, in a posture nearly double: they are below till the last hour of pregnancy, they have swelled haunches and ankles, and are prematurely brought to the grave, or, what is worse, a lingering existence . . . the state which the females are in after pulling like horses through these holes—their perspiration, exhaustion, and tears very frequently—it is painful in the extreme to witness it; yet when the work is done, they return to it with a vigour which is surprising, considering how they inwardly hate it."[1]

These were past horrors; those sturdy unladylike figures which we reproduce in No. 28 had been revealed to the public, and it had finally been shocked into social legislation. But that women were still capable of working long hours and had developed a surprising capacity for resisting exploitation must have been obvious to Miss Potter. For, in that survey of life and work in London which brought her into politics, there is a telling description of the energy, solidarity and high spirit of the

[1]Commission on the Employment of Women and Children in Mines and Factories, 1842 (quoted by Ray Strachey in *The Cause*).

London match girls. It was not an antifeminist movement, such as that which kept ladies out of the medical schools, which debarred women from employment in the mines, neither was it the feminists who kept them for long hours in the workshops of the East End. In fact women have never had the slightest difficulty in making their way into sweated industries. The champions of the home and sweet domesticity have usually regarded these unwomanly practices with considerable complacency. It would seem therefore that there was a certain inconsistency in the arguments of the antifeminists. But this inconsistency is more apparent than real, it was not "females" but ladies, whom they wished to restrain and to protect. If we accept the notion of Vicarious Consumption it at once becomes clear that a woman whose husband or parent has a reasonably large income is charged with a special duty; it is her business to be a parasite, and she fails in that mission if she provides for herself. By setting up as an independent producer she betrays the role which has been allotted her by Society.

When considered in this light the protests against the demand for women's rights appear perfectly reasonable. A man who uses his women as pegs on which to hang his trophies may justly be annoyed if they refuse to co-operate. They make him appear ridiculous and they are themselves, according to his definition, unfeminine. Of course there must always be females who have no social mission of this kind, and their labour is useful to the community; but they are differently constituted. They are not ladies. It is only if we refuse to accept the strictly economic and deeply class-conscious premises of this argument that it fails to convince.

The victory of the women over the ladies is due, primarily, to the decline in the Leisure Class itself. We can no longer make all the assumptions that were necessary to a whole-hearted acceptance of the doctrines of Vicarious Consumption. Moreover business men have found that women are useful, not only in mines and in factories, but in offices and in all kinds of clerical work. It was discovered that ladies could be tempted into employment and this was a most disruptive event. Finally there came the profoundly revolutionary necessities of two great wars.

War, when it is conducted on the modern scale, is as fatal to ornamental living as it is to ornamental soldiering. In the 1914-1918 war women were called into industry in great numbers (No. 141). They also forced their way into uniform and they diverted that ruthless energy and capacity for devoted action which had made the Suffrage Movement formidable, and the militants terrible, into a shrill and persistent patriotism which earned them the vote.

In the Second World War the services of women were more readily accepted and more quietly performed. Women—ladies too—had gone into action with Wellington's armies; but now, for the first time, they were conscripted (No. 171). In a war, the dangers of which were brought home to us, they found a natural place in what had become the front line.

Looking back one is astonished by the magnitude of the change that has taken place. And yet it is possible that we see the triumphs of feminism in too violent a perspective. We may fail to realise how much remains to be won. Also, in priding ourselves on the progress we have made, we may be tempted to exaggerate or even to idealise the empire of former habits. The indolence and passivity of the Nineteenth Century lady may have its charms for a generation which does its own housework, and the sentimentality of that tender age may now seem as pretty as wide skirts and poke bonnets. Thus we may construct a fashion-plate picture of the society which wept over Thackeray's Amelia and Dickens' Dora; in that picture the many formidable, businesslike and aggressive women who did not live in novels seem out of place. In fact the average lady must have been something between the normal heroine of fiction and the exceptional heroine of fact. Perhaps Surtees' portrait of Lady Main-chance (*née* Yammerton) comes as close to the truth as any. She was a very ladylike girl, modest, demure, ignorant and placidly determined to sell herself to the highest bidder.

IV

THE activities of ladies and gentlemen can be considered in isolation—up to a point. When that point is reached it becomes necessary to examine their joint activities; sex rears its ugly head and it is our duty to examine its salient features. The Mid-Nineteenth Century was peculiar in its attitude toward this subject. Judging by the literature of the age one might suppose that we are here confronted by an interlude as utterly remote from the world of Congreve and Wycherly as it is from that of D. H. Lawrence and James Joyce. This appearance is to some extent deceptive; the early Victorians were pompous, prudish and sanctimonious; but they accepted the values of their bawdy forefathers. The present age does not; it is unique in that it is improper without being naughty, for naughtiness—in this sense of the word—implies the recognition of rules. Dirt, whether it be moral or physical, is matter in the wrong place; in the Twentieth Century there is an ever increasing doubt as to which is the right place. One crucial example will show us the extent and nature of the revolution which has occurred.

In 1850, as in 1750 or 1650, it was supposed that a young girl could suffer no greater loss than that of her virtue; and by this was meant, not a spiritual or moral degradation, but a specific physical event. She might disobey her parents, blaspheme, pilfer, prevaricate, covet, break the sabbath, turn Buddhist, or even commit manslaughter without losing the hope of forgiveness; but that crime, which is not even referred to in the Decalogue, was unpardonable. The best that a young woman in this distressing predicament could do was to die of consumption—preferably on her father's doorstep.

A woman might marry a man whose principles, person and character she loathed, the possibility of such a union was the stock in trade of the Victorian novelist and his sympathies were always on the side of the marriage of affection; but it was never suggested that a marriage of convenience was utterly immoral. To the modern mind, a marriage without love seems more dishonourable than a marriage without virginity. The change of feeling has been immense, and perhaps we are sufficiently remote from the customs of our ancestors to be able to make an impartial enquiry into their motives.

The paramount importance of virginity is undoubtedly connected with many systems of magical and religious belief. The fact that the Victorians were more religious than we, may therefore be held to explain the precision of their views. Against this it must be said that a great many Victorians who rejected the dogma of religion accepted the current assumptions regarding feminine purity, and were as strict in their private lives as any Christians; also, a very little reflection must convince us that religious teachings, if strictly interpreted, have very little to do with the matter. To a sincerely religious person it must seem that a sin is a sin whoever commits it, and in the eyes of the Church—any Church—a youth who loses his innocence is quite as guilty as the woman with whom he loses it. "Flee fornication", said St Paul, and it was to the *gentlemen* of Corinth that he said it. But society takes a different view. The indiscretions of a young man might be censured by strict moralists; but they certainly did not spoil his chances of making a good marriage. Indeed, the principle of Conspicuous Consumption might be carried so far that a man would gain a certain credit by keeping a very expensive harlot. That which was a deadly sin on the part of one sex was accounted a venial error on the part of the other.

In fact, as has already been suggested, the social code of our ancestors was not wholly concerned with questions of morality. A woman was punished, perhaps not with the utmost severity, but still in a most unmistakable fashion, even when it was perfectly clear that she had remained entirely true to her principles. A Clarissa Harlowe might expect pity, but she could not expect a husband; she had, in the common phrase, been ruined. In much the same way a woman was punished for being the occasion of scandal, even when her character remained untouched. Lady Henry Somerset's only fault was that she married a husband afflicted by abnormalities of which, probably, she had never heard; nevertheless she was cut dead by 'society' when Lord Henry fled the country. Lady Millais, who was equally innocent, was excluded from the Queen's drawing rooms because she had annulled her marriage with Ruskin. In the same way all other wives who had committed the imprudence of being publicly wronged were shut out from Her Majesty's presence. In these matters our pious ancestors showed themselves exactly on a par with the most ignorant savages.

It is indeed difficult to find a rational motive in the workings of Victorian prudery. A young girl would certainly be told all about a contagious disease, such as scarlet fever, in order that she might protect herself from infection; but in the case of dangers which seemed much greater, she was disarmed by ignorance; and her ignorance, if we are to believe Mr Trollope, was stupendous. Apologising (in 1870) for the introduction of what he calls 'a castaway' in his novel *The Vicar of Bullhampton*, he writes thus:

"There arises, of course, the question whether a novelist, who professes to write for the amusement of the young of both sexes, should allow himself to bring upon his stage such a character . . . it is not long since—it is well within the recollection of the author—that the very existence of such a condition of life as was hers, was supposed to be unknown to our sisters and daughters, and was, in truth, unknown to many of them."

No doubt one could find many other examples; but this will suffice to show the oddity of a system in which young ladies were shielded from contact with—they knew not whom—in order that they might preserve—they knew not what.

And yet there is a further inconsistency to be mentioned, for it would be a mistake to imagine that this system of social conventions rested entirely upon the supposition that there is a special advantage to be gained by marrying a woman of spiritual and physical innocence. A well-provided widow never found any difficulty in obtaining a husband; the loss of her ignorance was no disadvantage to her. And a virtuous woman might lie with ten men in succession if she could account for them, in a satisfactory way, with certificates of marriage and of death.

It would appear, therefore, that this system of morality was based upon a belief in the sanctity of marriage and that that institution was, to a certain extent, separable from the ethical, religious, and thaumaturgic beliefs with which it has been so closely connected. Divorced from those beliefs it remains a legal and commercial relationship, in which the wife had been, and still was to a large extent, a form of property. Her imbecility, which deprived her of any legal rights and gave her no power over her children, enhanced her value as a vicarious consumer. Indeed her whole position as a pure consumer, her value as an instrument for displaying status, depended upon the assumption that she was the property of her parent or her husband.

A scandal before marriage was therefore a disaster, because it deprived a woman of her full market value and made it seem that she had become, as one may say, 'socialised'. Since marriage was a contract, which could hardly be ended save by the death of one of the contracting parties, a woman could only become polyandrous by burying a succession of husbands; and, since a man belonged, as it were, to himself alone, his extra-marital adventures were of no consequence. Adultery, on the same reckoning, becomes, and is in law, a species of theft. It was thought a much more serious crime for a man to steal another man's wife than for him to enjoy public property. Parnell was much more blamed for seducing Mrs O'Shea than was Lord Hartington for keeping Skittles.

A man who robs is universally condemned; but the fool who is cozened is an object of ridicule. This may account for the fact that improper behaviour was a less tragic affair for a married woman than for a girl. A married woman was, to some extent, protected by her husband's vanity and fear of ridicule; and a cynical or tolerant husband might connive at his wife's infidelities, so long as they were accomplished in a discreet manner. But it is one thing to accept a certain amount of short measure, quite another to see one's goods spoilt before they have reached the market. Few Victorian parents, however broad-minded, would have been willing to see their daughters enjoy that licence which was granted to young men.

It would appear then that the seeming contradictions of that system of sexual morality, which had endured from time immemorial until the latter half of the last century, can be resolved if we admit that women were movable property. The innovation of the Nineteenth Century was the additional importance accorded to ignorance and to modesty. No doubt this was in part caused by the rise of a new class greatly interested in questions of property and having no aristocratic tradition of gallantry and cynicism. I think we may also ascribe it to the increasingly important part played by women in the business of Conspicuous Consumption. As men turned more and more to active and industrious ways of life it became increasingly important that their wives and daughters should be imbecile, innocent and inefficient. The

C

busyness of men made the ornamental character of women more important than ever; and a woman had no ornament more precious than her virtue.

The system began to break down when ladies enforced their right to be treated as autonomous individuals, consumers in their own right, creatures who could make money and waste it for themselves. Those who opposed feminine education, and who attempted to prevent women from entering the professions, were too polite to assert that women, being furniture, could have no rights and should have no feelings. Probably they would have been shocked by such a statement of their position; nevertheless their assertion that a woman's proper place is in the home involved assumptions of this nature. The argument that the emancipation of women would end by destroying the family rested upon the same proprietary notion. In view of all that has happened since emancipation, it is hard to deny that these forebodings seem to have been justified. For although nothing was further from the minds of the original feminists, who saw in women the incorruptible guardians of innocence and of virtue, it cannot be said that the patriarchal morality of our grand-parents has been replaced by a new morality in which both sexes are confined by those severe laws to which women alone were subject. Man-made morality, resting upon the sanctity of the family and the provision of whores, of which Mr Lecky was so eloquent an advocate, was, not unnaturally, the target of the feminists of an older generation; they believed that when women had political power a greater and more equal measure of chastity would be imposed, and they placed themselves at the head of all movements which aimed at the reduction of licence and the punishment of vice. It is probable that some of their adversaries found nothing more alarming in the Suffrage Movement than the uncompromising puritanism of its exponents. It now seems quite certain that their fears were groundless.

Before examining what appear to be the fruits of the feminist victories it may be helpful to glance at two important crises in the struggle for equality. The first turning point came in the 'seventies, when the great landowning aristocrats came to the end of their long period of affluence. In those years the cheap and mechanised farming of the New World began to produce grain in great quantities and new methods of refrigeration brought cheap foreign meat into our markets. For the first time the British aristocracy began to complain of poverty. Another and different kind of importation did something to mend matters, for it was about this time that young Americans, of considerable charm and great wealth, began to marry into our upper classes. The acceptance of these heiresses resulted from the action of many causes, of which the agricultural depression was but one; but undoubtedly something drastic had happened to alter the opinions of the governing classes in this country. The society which welcomed the 'American Invasion' with such whole-hearted enthusiasm had not always been so friendly to the noisily democratic republic on the other side of the Atlantic. It is curious to compare the attitude, which was now adopted, with the virulent hatred and abuse of the Yankees which was almost universal in good society at the time of the Civil War, a war which had been welcomed because it was believed that it marked the end of the Union and the downfall of Democracy. That had been in 1861, in twenty years opinions had changed, or the terms on which dollars were offered for titles had proved irresistible.

So many great English families allied themselves with the wealth and beauty of the United States that the habits of the upper classes were profoundly affected. The invaders were able to impose their own standards; they met their husbands' society with many advantages, their romantic snobbery was qualified by the practical iconoclasm of a superbly confident plutocracy; the audacity of their innocence confounded Mrs Grundy, and they were armed with the vigorous feminine egotism of a land where all social affairs are in the hands of women. The tedium, rigidity and brutality of Victorian life was broken by their assault. "They insisted", writes one contemporary observer, "on being amused. Dancing, bridge and games of every description replaced the old somnolent evenings."[1]

They did more; they introduced the moral standards of a nation which produced young women of a type which is now sufficiently familiar; but which was then astonishingly new.

"They are self-possessed without parting with any tenderness that is their sex-right; they understand; they can take care of themselves; they are superbly independent. When you ask them what makes them so charming, they say: 'It is because we are better educated than your girls and we are more sensible in regard to men. We have good times all round, but we aren't taught to regard every man as a possible husband. Nor is he expected to marry the first girl he calls on regularly.' Yes, they have good times, their freedom is large, and they do not abuse it. They can go driving with young men and receive visits from young men to an extent that would make an English mother wink with horror; and neither the driver nor the drivee have a thought beyond the enjoyment of a good time."[2]

The example of young women such as these made the entire Victorian conception of maidenly behaviour seem ridiculous. Their presence, whether as tourists or as wives subverted the entire patriarchal pattern of decorum. They made feminine freedom respectable, for they were good girls; their behaviour was widely imitated, for they were a social success.

The second great event in a process which, it must be realised, was continuous, was the war of 1914. We have already mentioned the economic and political changes which that conflict produced in the status of women. After the war women could no longer be expected to play their part in a scheme of things in which it was assumed that they were creatures of no importance. They had discovered the pleasures, not only of liberty, but of licence. The war had encouraged young men and women to short-circuit the obstacles of a moral code which was too cumbrous to meet the needs of those who lived in imminent expectation of death. The young men went out to join the enormous casualty lists; the young women whom they left behind

[1]The Earl of Middleton in *Fifty Years*.

[2]Kipling. *From Sea to Sea*, Chap. xxv. Kipling was observing life in California in the eighteen-eighties.

them produced 'war-babies'. There was an outburst of extravagant behaviour which continued after the war and has been excellently described in the American phrase 'sleeping around'; it was crowned by that supreme manifestation of feminine emancipation: the gigolo.

If the noisy licence of the 'bright young people' now seems rather *demodé*, the moral assumptions on which it was based remain. In achieving liberty woman has become her own mistress and the mistress of anyone else with whom she may come to an understanding; with the decline in the older notions of property and, above all, with the invention of efficient contraceptives, this attitude is no longer penalised by public opinion or economic disadvantages. It has become sufficiently common for young people to live together before marriage for the practice to excite hardly any comment, or, at all events, far less than would have seemed possible, eighty years ago; and when people do marry they are not reluctant to dissolve the union if they find that it makes both parties miserable. While all polyandrous or polygamous adventures cause far less fuss than they once did, extra-marital adventures and disappointments are thought less important than the convulsions of married couples, in that they tend to produce less side-taking and back-biting among the friends of the principals and do not involve those painful readjustments which are frequent when children are involved in a separation.

It may be said that these changes involve no more than a minority of the nation, and that the great majority continues to follow the traditional pattern of social behaviour. This is true; but the minority is not insignificant and it is increasing and increasingly influential. Its influence is reflected in the more frank and tolerant attitude towards sexual matters which is now evident in nearly all that is said and written on this subject.

It may, therefore, appear that those who maintained that 'family life' would suffer if women were emancipated have been justified by the transformations of the past eighty years. But it is at least arguable that we are not confronted by a cause and an effect, but by two aspects of the same process. The patriarchal morality of our forefathers was, as I have tried to suggest, a proprietory morality and, when the sanctity of property itself was no longer acknowledged, the liberties and the licence of the present age became possible. The diminishing role of children and servants in the business of Vicarious Consumption, and the fact that the 'master of the house' has changed his attitude, not only to his wife, but to these other dependants, suggests a very wide development which has affected, and may entirely transform, the structure of the household. With no firm belief in the authority of religious leaders, in the sacred rights of private property, or in the superior status of husbands and fathers, it is difficult to see how the family, as we have known it, can survive. Whether that secular institution can, in some way, be recreated upon a basis of affection, expediency and tolerance, remains to be seen.

V

FROM their dizzy social eminence, the ladies and gentlemen of a hundred years ago may sometimes have noticed the strange and monstrous creatures who inhabited the deepest abyss of society and, if they looked with sufficient attention, they may have perceived a dark and unpleasing image of themselves. Among the criminal and near-criminal elements there was a kind of mock-leisure class peopled by roughs, bullies, panders, tricksters, etc., men who supported themselves by more or less predatory activities, who amused themselves by drinking—as the saying is—'like lords', and by wagering on dogs and horses. They settled their disputes by some rude form of duel and disdained the ignoble virtues of the thrifty, the industrious and the respectable.

If the rowdy provides us with a caricature of the gentleman, the harlot—his natural companion—is, even more clearly, an obscene variety of the lady. In the higher ranks of her profession she was hardly to be distinguished from her virtuous sisters, and even the pavement drab dressed and behaved in half conscious parody of the Leisure Class proper.

This lower class was a nuisance, but not a menace, to society. In fact it was, in its way, a stabilising influence. It is the sober industrious artisan or labourer who subverts the social order and provides the revolutionary solidarity of the masses. Your criminal or semi-criminal type is a fierce individualist, a traditionalist, naturally respectful to the gentry, easily shocked, and a firm believer in that patriarchal system of morals which, as we have seen, allows a proper sphere of action for the rake and his doxy. The women in particular are perfectly submissive to all supernatural powers, super-stition and bigotry may be classed among the occupational diseases of prostitution. The men tend to leave the business of religion to their women; the same tendency may be observed in the upper classes.

The socially acquiescent enemy of society is still a normal phenomenon of our 'underworld' and perhaps his conservatism is an inevitable outcome of his manner of life; but he was more obviously a part of the social system at a time when the 'regime of status' was still intact, for that regime provided a well-marked station in life for everyone in the community, even for the public enemies. Then, every social stratum had its own manners, dress, speech and moral standards. Fashion in dress was a barely perceptible influence in the lower classes, so that there was much more variety from class to class than there is now and much less variety from year to year.

Something of this rigid caste system still remained in the England of 1850, although it was fast dying. It was still possible to tell a sailor from a carpenter and a farmer from a farm labourer, and this, even when they were dressed in their best. In the case of the women of the lower and lower middle classes there was already more uniformity; for they were curiously placed. They had no traditional dress and were therefore free to follow the fashion but, on the other hand, they could not emulate the dress of high society, partly because it was far too expensive, and partly

because the women who did wear a meretricious travesty of that style were not respectable. Thus they contented themselves with a certain quiet and unpretending neatness of attire.

What we have here said of dress is largely true of the manners, customs, furnishing and speech of those classes which followed a traditional occupation. There were refinements of taste that would have been thought absurd in a sea captain, accomplishments which would have been considered forward and unbecoming in a farmer's daughter. The middle classes had to walk between the nice limits of disreputability and swank, they had, in a word, to know their place.

It was the newer professions, those which had no place in the regime of status, which were keenest in emulating the upper classes; it was not a matter of choice but of necessity. They were obliged to follow the fashion on pain of being thought contemptible. In the underpaid but genteel professions emulation caused the greatest hardship; the clerk and the shopwalker were compelled by their business to associate with wealthy people and were practically forced to live beyond their means. They had to appear neat and spotless at their place of work and the new suburban house had to be furnished and maintained in a manner which would keep up appearances.

On the Day Of Rest the apparatus of leisure was particularly elaborate and the observance of social duties more than usually important. Conspicuous Consumption in Church has always been a characteristic of Western Christianity. A parade to and from the place of worship, exceptionally expensive and uncomfortable clothes, family bibles and prayer books of sumptuous but funereal design, unusually large meals and unusually boring conversation, pious occupations and decorous social gatherings, desperate attempts to keep the children in a state of decent idleness, a rigorous abstention from all useful or amusing occupations, such were the features of the English Sabbath in the last century. It was a festival of Conspicuous Consumption and Conspicuous Leisure performed in honour of Our Lord through the medium of social ostentation.

The great advantage of Sunday, from the point of view of the lower and lower middle classes, was that it gave an opportunity for the display of accumulated savings in the form of 'Sunday best'. It provided an opportunity for the working man to prove his latent capacities and to be, for one day out of the seven, a gentleman. The sabbath was therefore a day of exhibition and innovation; it was then that the maid tried out her new bonnet while the butcher's boy sported some new audacity in cravats. As time went on these adventures became more and more daring; not that millinery and haberdashery were more colourful and grotesque, but that those who wore them belonged to lower and lower strata of society and therefore gave evidence of greater and greater impudence. In fact the regime of status was in a decline and uniformity was gaining ground. One by one the older trades lost their traditional distinctions; the great towns and the industrial districts led the way; but in the end even the countryman's smock was driven into remote districts and at last extinguished.

INTRODUCTION

In his *Principles of Economics* Alfred Marshall tells us that: "In Scotland . . . in Adam Smith's time many persons were allowed by custom to go abroad without shoes and stockings who may not do so now; and many still do it in Scotland who might not in England. Again, in England now a well-to-do labourer is expected to appear on Sunday in a black coat and, in some places, in a silk hat; though these would have subjected him to ridicule but a short time ago. There is a constant increase both in that variety and expensiveness which custom requires as a minimum, and in that which it tolerates as a maximum; and the efforts to obtain distinction by dress are extending themselves throughout the lower grades of English society."

Marshall's observations were made before 1890; twenty years later the process was nearing completion. Oswald Barron notes that: ". . . the town dress of London or Paris is imitated by all peoples and by rich and poor. Especially is this the case in England where the clean and honourable blouse of the French workman is not, a journeyman painter or labourer often going to his work in a frayed and greasy morning coat after the cut of that in which a rich man will pay a London morning call."[1]

The lower classes have been demanding the right to look like their 'betters' ever since the end of the Middle Ages (we must note in passing that the 'demand', as Marshall shows, may also be expressed as a compulsion), the concession of that claim has been very gradual and the full Industrial reponse to the new market thus created is very recent. The fashion paper, the pattern, the sewing machine, new cheap textiles and mass production have made the popular desire to dress the part more nearly attainable. The clothes of the English working woman are no longer that 'frowsy parody of richer women's frippery' which shocked observant foreigners two generations ago.[2]

A house is, in the nature of things, more difficult to adapt for the purposes of ostentation than is a dress. England has always abounded in houses which could not, by any effort of ingenuity, be made to appear decent. But in the furnishing of a house a substantial effort in this direction can be made. In many small cottages the visitor will find one room which is frankly devoted to Conspicuous Consumption. It is a parlour and, like the front door, it is never used. The family lives in the kitchen, which is warm in winter and convenient in summer; here the table is covered with an oil cloth, the chairs have been worn down to a certain slovenly comfort, and here are the children, the cat and the radio. The parlour, on the other hand, is a shrine inhabited by the Household Gods; here the furniture is both elegant and uncomfortable, the stuffed pheasant in its glass case is carefully preserved from harm, and the treasures of successive generations are dusted, polished and displayed. Here one may find sentimental mid-Victorian conceits, such as the fragile and tortuous china of the 'sixties and 'seventies (No. 42), the accumulated knick-knacks of a later period and perhaps some dated relics: a chromolithograph of Holman Hunt's *Light of the World*, to which a more daring generation has added one of Lord Leighton's public

[1] See *Encyclopaedia Britannica*, XIth ed. Article on Costume.   [2] Ibid.

33

baths, a Japanese fan which has crept hither from Kensington via some great country house, a tastefully bound volume of Omar Khayyam and, finally, a gaudy cushion, the harsh geometrical pattern of which derives, at five hundred removes, from Braque and from Picasso.

The greater part of this collection, if exhibited to a discerning critic of the upper classes, would produce horror, pity or ridicule. The more recent acquisitions would be felt to be exceptionally disgusting. The inevitable verdict would be that the collector—that is to say a large section of the working class—is devoid of taste.

Now, judgments of this nature imply a good deal more than is commonly realised. Where the working man buys, and is content, with a poor copy of an original, a case can be made against his taste; but in the applied arts and literature, where all classes enjoy substantially the same æsthetic opportunities, it is impossible to pass judgment on the proclivities of the lower classes without condemning their 'betters'.

It is hardly necessary to call in evidence the æsthetic history of the past hundred years in order to make a point which is, it must be allowed, sufficiently trite. But a brief examination of the mechanism whereby æsthetic modes are generated, diffused, and vulgarised may confirm and amplify the argument. This mechanism is substantially similar to the ordinary process of emulation, to which reference has already been made. In the history of costume, which provides the most striking and typical examples of fashionable change, the process may be summarised thus: the upper classes adopt a new style and, in so doing, make it socially reputable. It is then imitated by all those who desire to be socially reputable and this, in modern societies, means everyone. When the style (or variant of a style) has been universally adopted it has been made common, because it is common socially reputable people are no longer willing to wear it, they must therefore adopt another style which immediately undergoes the same process. Thus, because diffusion engenders aversion, the clothes of a community such as ours are in a state of perpetual change which we call 'fashion'.

In much the same way, though to a lesser extent, a new book, a new painter, a new decorative style, a new religion, or a new philosophy may be taken up, not so much for its intrinsic merits, but on account of its novelty, and, having been accepted, it also will be diffused, vulgarised and discarded.

There is however a break on this process which delays, and may even prevent, its action. Those who are content with the existing state of things, and the leaders of fashion are likely to belong to that class, will probably mistrust a proposal which involves any kind of social change; for them any change must be a change for the worse. Even so harmless an innovation as the crinoline or the 'new look' offends the natural conservatism of a great part of society; and naturally, this objection applies with much greater force to a new idea, or a new aesthetic, which may even carry a suggestion of political change.

Nevertheless, the most disquieting doctrines and habits sometimes make their way into a section of good society and, in their slower, more limited fashion, descend the social scale as though they had been bonnets or bustles.

34

These ideological fashions are made possible by yet another countervailing influence. If one wishes to avoid liking that which everyone likes, it is necessary to cultivate a taste for that which is unpopular. It is better to be eccentric, peculiar, or even repellant, than to be vulgar. The vicious and scandalous conduct of the Victorian gentleman, which has already been referred to, was, in part, a means to this end; it distinguished the nobleman from the tradesman. In rather the same way we find that well bred people of our own time use a coarser language than that which is usual in the lower middle classes. A gentleman will sweat and take a napkin to wipe the spittle off his belly, while his inferior perspires and takes a serviette to wipe the saliva off his abdomen. In both cases we find a privileged class joining hands with the lowest ranks in order to circumvent the bourgeoisie.

The use of aesthetic nonconformity to attain social distinction is less obviously an affair of fashion; nevertheless the same social process appears to be at work. The Pre-Raphaelites were considered the most reckless innovators when they started the Brotherhood; to admire them showed singular refinement and, in consequence, it was not long before they were generally admired; they became the fashion, they were knighted, canonised, popularised and, in due course, shelved. Their successors, the aesthetes, were saved from a like fate by eccentricities of conduct which went a little too far for prevailing canons of taste and morality, and which ended, disastrously, in the Wilde scandal. But the pure and high-minded innovators of the New English Art Club were able to repeat the social success of the Pre-Raphaelites with precisely the same results. In our own time we have seen the same process of revulsion, social success and vulgarisation in the history of the Post Impressionists who, having been received with horror by the cultivated public, were accepted by the same public as something smartly daring, were made the fashion, and have now become public property. Finally we may observe how the wheel has come full circle bringing the early and mid-Victorians back to favour, so that our modern critics are able to go into raptures over such trifles as "The Source of England's Greatness" (No. 36) admiration for such works has for so long been unfashionable as to become eccentric, and thus fashionable once more.

The fact that an aesthetic admiration is assisted by the desire for social distinction does not mean that the admirer does not feel a real sentiment, when confronted by the works of art which happen to be in vogue. To suppose this is to suppose an almost inconceivable degree of hypocrisy. A style or an artist is past reason hunted; and no sooner had, past reason hated—and both sentiments are perfectly sincere. In examining that photograph which shows us the feminine mode of the year 1928 (No. 150) we can prove in our own persons the reality of these phenomena. Those who are old enough to remember the fashions of that year will remember also that, at that time, they were charming. To-day they are grotesque. With the photographic evidence before us it is clear that beauty lies in the eye of the beholder; we have been subjected to a social force which has deranged our aesthetic emotions. The same is true, though in lesser degree, of those who rejected, then admired, and finally laughed at the paintings of Holman Hunt. The evidence leads us to speculations too far-reaching for an essay of this kind, and no doubt our generalisations would require considerable modification if they were to be made the basis for an aesthetic theory; it must, for instance, be remembered that paintings, like clothes, can be more accurately assessed at an historic distance, when the immediate social impulses have been withdrawn. But, when this has been said it remains true that aesthetic phenomena are closely connected with the processes of social change; and that to criticise a class or an individual for admiring something which has, in course of time, become ugly and ridiculous amounts, in effect, to saying that one is only justified in liking the fashion at the moment when it is fashionable. It would be about as sensible to reproach a fish for not giving suck to its young.

There is this to be added, if the picture of the aesthetic behaviour of the nation is to be made complete, that the lower and lower middle classes are much more sensitive to aesthetic needs than are the upper and upper middle classes. For, if we accept the view that the desire to be fittingly adorned and to live in properly decorated surroundings is an aesthetic desire, and it is hard to see how else it is to be defined, then it is clear, from what has already been said, that the lower classes devote more time, more money and more care to making themselves and their surroundings beautiful than do those groups which are socially secure. Proportionately the difference is enormous for, in the lower classes, and especially in the lower middle classes, material wants, and even the most elementary needs of the body, are sacrificed in order to present a decent appearance. Comparable sacrifices are not made by the upper income groups in the cause of Art.

It is among those of us who are socially insecure that the pursuit of distinction and respectability is most earnestly pursued; a lax and indifferent attitude towards social duties is only possible where some other quality makes such effort unnecessary; there are few who can afford the unaffected shabbiness, meanness and incivility of a great aristocrat. We are constrained by the laws of Conspicuous Consumption and Conspicuous Waste to spend some time, thought and money on being polite, well-dressed, decently furnished and sufficiently alert to be able to talk about the right films or novels, pictures, plays and people.

Our social duties start at the moment when we are told to mitigate our noisy demands for cake with a polite formula; thereafter we become conscious of a multitude of demands and prohibitions, all of which derive from the inexorable laws of 'good form'. The miserable perplexities of the new boy at school, who uses the wrong slang or offends some established totem, are reinforced by a reasonable terror of his little playmates; but when their violent sanctions have been removed we still have a lively social conscience which is ever ready to admonish us. This vigilant censor is ready to point to every spot of grease, every riding tie, every slipping petticoat, every dropped H or imperfect vowel of which we may be guilty. It wakes us up in the small hours with a brisk reminder that we once solemnly pronounced a Beaujolais to be the best claret we had ever tasted, and that we then drank it from a champagne glass;

also that we had been under the impression that Jean Francois Millet was the painter of ''Bubbles''; also that, when the vicar came to call he found our youngest daughter sitting on her chamber pot and singing ''Frankie and Johnnie'' at the top of her voice; also—but there is no point in accumulating social agonies which, in one form or another, must be tolerably familiar to the reader.

Social misadventures have always been obvious material for the humorist. This is strikingly exemplified in old volumes of Punch, where Du Maurier has depicted the endless perplexities of the middle classes. Again and again we find jokes which turn upon the fact that vulgar people do not know how to behave in polite society. Terrible children reveal the social pretensions of their shoddy parents; ambition is snubbed, aesthetic fashions are derided and the endless adventure of Mrs Ponsonby de Tompkyns in her search for lions continues from number to number. The same material is used by more serious artists in a dozen different manners but, nearly always, until Mr H. G. Wells arose as the prophet of the lower middle classes, the subject was approached from above, and our sympathies are on the side of polite society.

In *Kipps* and, to a lesser extent, in *Tono Bungay*, Wells drew a picture of the agonies of the social intruder as seen from *his* point of view. In so doing he was able to draw on his own experience and the result is memorable and convincing. It marks, also, an important stage in the development of our modern society and in the decline of the regime of status. The Edwardian era had begun and, in that age of social decomposition the masses were ceasing to be respectful and the classes were ceasing to be respectable.

The death of Queen Victoria and the accession of Edward VII was accompanied by a revolution in manners which may be likened, superficially, to the change which followed the death of Louis XIV. In both cases a long reign ended in disillusion and discomfiture, an old and pious monarch was succeeded by a middle-aged voluptuary; rank was submerged by wealth and moral earnestness by moral laxity. Now an aristocracy, if it is to survive, must remain in every way respectable; it must be stern and unbending in all things. The Edwardians were not.

The abandonment of traditional standards of sexual morality has already been discussed, and in part explained; here I want only to call attention to the effect of this abandonment on the popular acceptance of the regime of status. There can be little doubt that the rigid morality of Queen Victoria helped to save the monarchy in the Nineteenth Century, and the libertinism of the Edwardian Age was still of a sufficiently patriarchal character to leave the monarchy almost untouched; but the Kings entourage could not escape so easily. It was bent on pleasure and it needed money; the monarch chose his friends from the ranks of the new plutocracy, without regard to status. In seeking amusement society trembled on the verge of tolerance; its intrigues were still covert, but the savage denunciations, the intolerant holiness, the pitiless social ostracism of the past, was giving place to a smart and flippant cynicism. If they had not been so decidedly vulgar and so completely philistine, the

37

Edwardian magnates might have resembled their ancestors of the Eighteenth Century.

The exemplary life of King George V and of our present King have restored whatever may have been lost during the short reign of Edward VII; but the nobility is less continent and has less social security so that, to-day, its scandals and its less dignified activities are too familiar to be remarkable. The loss of status which accompanied this change is very marked; but the status of the Crown remains unimpaired and, when Edward VIII attempted to apply what are now the usual aristocratic standards of conduct to his own domestic arrangements, he at once discovered that the popularity of the Monarchy depends upon a patriarchal conception of royal behaviour. The King can no more marry a divorced woman than he can open his palace to paying guests, or become a guinea-pig director.

While the upper classes have, so to speak, unbent and lowered themselves in the eyes of the masses, the common people, on their side, have quickened the pace of emulation to a point at which it becomes very difficult to maintain class distinctions. In this the Labour Movement of the past seventy years has played a considerable part. The cultural influence of that movement is a subject which deserves more attention than it has received. The work of the pioneers of Socialism has—intentionally or not—included much more than a process of political indoctrination. It spread new literary and artistic ideas and, in so doing, it was aided by that process of emulation which has already been described.

From the first the movement was inspired by artists, the revival of the eighties was intimately connected with Morris and the Pre-Raphaelites and, at a later stage, with the 'New Theatre' of Ibsen and the 'New Music' of Wagner as explained by Bernard Shaw. To the intelligent artisan, intent on bettering himself intellectually, such a mixture seemed nicely compounded of socially acceptable and economically desirable ingredients. He would have been shocked by the atheistical materialism of the Marxists; but the high-minded intellectual and moral nonconformity of Wells and Shaw and the Webbs was less alarming in itself, and was often recommended by being presented in an aesthetic and socially reputable form.

The effect of this teaching has been to create a permanent demand for aesthetic and intellectual enlightenment on the part of a class which was totally indifferent to such things eighty years ago. Those who have lectured to Left Book Clubs or Fabian Societies will have noticed how strongly this desire persists.

Of course the Socialist Groups were but one of the media through which this hunger for culture expressed itself. Their work would have been impossible without free education, cheap books and cheap reproductions, and to-day the demand is more general, also, the supply is more adequate. Modern Science, by giving us the Wireless and the Cinema has enormously increased the speed at which new ideas can be disseminated. The Wireless has already been in existence for a sufficient length of time for a perceptible change in musical taste to have become remarkable.

The Cinema which, unlike broadcasting, is largely an importation, has been made to serve social demands of a much cruder nature than those which we have been discussing. The film is an incomparable medium for the satisfaction of two very deep human desires. It provides what, in former times, was supplied by the Church, the Court and the Stage, that is to say: a romantic and luxurious parade of wealth and power. To return to the Veblenian phraseology, the makers of films consume vicariously on our behalf. As though to emphasise this side of their activities they are always eager to let us know how much they do consume; how many millions were devoted to the production of such and such a film, what extravagant demands were made by the leading ladies and gentlemen, what millions of supers were engaged to swell the crowds, what cities were built to be destroyed for our entertainment. All this magnificently reckless spending is caught in the lens and made luminous upon the screen of our local cinema; we are presented with the shadow of more prodigious spectacles than have ever been staged. Now whereas the display of ecclesiastical, public or theatrical wealth ministers to our self importance in that we are, in some sort, the employers of our Church, our Court and our Theatre, the film adds pomp and circumstance to our private dreams and desires; it is a far more intimate medium than is the theatre, for it takes us across the footlights and, where the stage shows us individuals at a distance, the cinema leads us to a more intimate vision, showing us Nero through Poppæa's eyes and Poppæa through Nero's. Thus, by an easy flight of the imagination, we are allowed to replace the actors. If we are gentlemen we can set fire to Rome and fiddle while the city burns; if we are ladies we can enjoy a bath of asses' milk; and if we are Christians we may fancy ourselves devoured by lions. In fact we are provided with an art which combines the most lavish of spectacles with the seductive magic of the novelette.

The day-dream life of the cinema should provide useful evidence regarding the social ideals and aspirations of the masses. It is however necessary to remember that most films are made six thousand miles from London and are intended for a market which stretches from Tierra del Fuego to Reykjavik. Those moving pictures of English life which show our feudal aristocracy and its crenellated baronial strongholds, the servile peasantry, the old family retainers, and hounds meeting in the glory of a June morning, are to be treated with reserve.

Native productions give a rather different impression and, in so far as we can assess the condition of public taste from this class of evidence, we may suppose that the more naive forms of emulation have been discarded. The regime of status is very much weakened. The more blatant day dreams of rank and privilege are confined to the realms of historical romance. Indeed, in so far as the present age is concerned, there is a certain reticence about mentioning the facts of class. This pudicity may also be observed in our everyday language; the upper and lower classes are no longer referred to as such; we speak of "the upper and lower income groups", or find some other decent euphemism. The same tendency may be observed in our advertisements; where a former generation found it sufficient to recommend a product with the simple phrase: "as supplied to the nobility and gentry", this modern age does no more than suggest that the users of—whatever it may be—wear expensive clothes and speak in a fashionable slang. It is true that Lady Blank allows her perfect features to be photographed, and assures the readers of the popular press that the brilliance of her eyes is entirely due to an unremitting use of Parthian Eyewash; but such advertisements are far less common than they used to be. Those engrossing stories which tell us how people who stink, or stutter, or fall short of social perfection in some other way, thus ruining their romances and business careers (until everything is put right by the advice of a candid friend and they live happily ever after, thanks to someone's elixir) are set in quite humble surroundings inhabited by simple, kindly, handsome, credulous members of the upper or lower middle classes. All of which suggests that the regime of status, if not dead, is passing through anxious moments, which call for hushed voices and discreet circumlocutions.

Under the circumstances the present condition of the Leisure Class appears both delicate and interesting. It continues to fight an unequal battle for social distinction; but it no longer has the reserves on which it could once depend. To some extent it is obliged to adopt that system of occasional display which has for long been used by the lower classes. Thus it can drop all pretence of leisure for considerable periods and then, when its resources are adequate, it can blossom out in satin and white waistcoats. At the same time increasing use is made of the weapons of superior culture—as, for instance, of up-to-date information concerning the arts; these methods of ostentation require less ready cash than most others, and are much more widely used than they were two generations ago. By methods such as these it is at least possible to preserve a class which keeps a semblance of the leisured way of life; nevertheless it is doubtful whether they can suffice in the long run. The whole tendency of the social and political development of the past hundred years has been towards an obliteration of class distinctions, to an ever-increasing rapidity in the process of emulation and to a progressive weakening of the regime of status.

VI

IN these pages I have tried to remain as objective and as uncritical as the photographs that are before you. My purpose has been to suggest what seems to me a useful approach to the social history of the past hundred years; and in such an endeavour it would be very improper to confuse the functions of the observer with those of the moralist. I am well aware that certain critics will find fault with such an attitude; they will consider that I have failed to realise the vast opportunities which a survey of this kind provides for the exhibition of righteous indignation. The extinction of all that is charming, innocent and ancient in the social habits of our country, the steady growth of vulgarity, the decay of social distinctions, in a word, the decline of the Leisure Class, might well have been deplored if I had had the inclination to deplore it. On the other hand there is in these pages a grand but unexploited theme for social wrath. The spectacle of a society so arranged that the great mass of the people was kept in the dreariest surroundings and engaged on the most laborious tasks, in order that a small and selfish group of parasites might have the dubious pleasure of making itself expensively miserable, invites the censorious pen. I leave all such reflections to my readers; they are quite capable of drawing whatever moral they may think appropriate. It is my business to give them a few of the facts on which to base their judgments and to suggest some of the motives from which those facts result.

It may however be said, that in attempting to examine the past without playing the part of an advocate, I have fallen into an error of equal magnitude and have adopted the foolish role of the superficial buffoon. Certainly it is easy to raise a cheap laugh at the expense of our forefathers and to exploit the fact that those social regulations which we no longer respect always appear somewhat ridiculous. It must be allowed that such proceedings do not show a very advanced stage of reflection or of humour. But if, as I hope that I have shown, the absurdities of the past are the expression of social laws which still operate today, then we may perhaps learn to understand, and even to sympathise, with follies which were imposed by strong social necessities. A philosopher may smile at the gothic pretensions of the chair on which the bishop of Durham is seated (No. 38); but he will find it no more absurd than the spurious half timbering of British Railways (No. 188).

An attempt to examine the nature and workings of those laws of display which were first described by Veblen cannot but appear to be an attempt to make grand things look ridiculous. This danger is increased when we try to anatomize the manners and follies of a particular age; for that which is abnormal must always appear more comic than that which is normal. It is therefore worth while to point out that we are here dealing with an aspect of human behaviour which recurs continually throughout the history of man. When a Celtic chieftain died, his chariots, his horses with all their rich harness, his jewels, his weapons and his slaves were buried with him. There is evidence of the same lavish waste in the burial habits of most other peoples from

41

China to Egypt. No one, except the archæologists (whose interests were not envisaged) could profit from Conspicuous Waste of this kind. In much the same way we find that nearly all the great monuments of the Middle Ages and of the Ancient World were built to serve non-industrial ends. It may be argued that the great cathedrals and temples were erected, not to the glory of man but to that of his Maker; but it is hard to disentangle the motives of piety from those of ostentation. What, for instance, are we to say in the case of a poor Londoner of the last century, who would spend all her savings on burying her husband with decent pomp? Such cases were not uncommon and are still to be found. Can it be that a sincere Christian supposes that the soul of the departed stands a worse chance on the last day if the body arises from a pauper's grave? The demands of Conspicuous Consumption are involved with our holiest, our most intimate, beliefs and feelings.

A belief in the value of Conspicuous Leisure is no less general. The classic example comes from the other side of the earth where Chinese women endure unspeakable agonies, compressing their feet in order that they may be unable to walk. But a Chinese author[1] is able to retort with the following extract from a European fashion journal:

"When lacing the new stays, the young lady should lie face downwards on her bedroom floor, and her mother should place her foot in the small of her daughter's back in order to obtain a good purchase. There should then be no difficulty in making the stays meet."

In both cases society and the victim herself accept the practice of deformation without protest. Nor can we condemn such practices by reference to the undefinable criterion of 'common sense'; it may be common sense to avoid pain and ill-health, but is it not also common sense to satisfy one's own vanity, to gain the admiration of others, and perhaps, to secure material advantages by means of tiny feet or a trim waist? Probably, as is the case with most social observances, the victim complies without question; it is taken for granted that one accepts the habits of one's class and age. Within its own conventions society has its own common sense and its own morality; and if society demands that gentlemen's gentlemen should be buried when their master dies, or that a well brought up young woman should deform her feet, or that no gentleman shall shoot a fox, then society, within its own limitations, is right. It is, however, necessary to remember that the taboos of the Celt and the Mandarin are just as respectable as those of the squire.

The peculiar interest of the squire (and hence of our period) lies in the fact that he is less self-assured, more complex, and more changeable than the oriental or the barbarian. He belongs to a social system which is fundamentally unstable, which produces critics and rebels, and which boxes the compass in response to the varying winds of fashion. Thus the European lady who tries to abolish her belly has less excuse, if excuse be needed, than her Chinese sister who can at least say: "I do no more than my ancestors have done for a thousand years." The European lady who finds her portrait

[1]Lin Yutang. *My Country, My People.*

amongst the later pages of this book will experience something between amusement and horror; for to that odd feeling which is produced by the image of ourselves as we once were, will be added the still more curious experience of seeing ourselves dressed in fashions which have ceased to charm.

Fashion shows us the world through a distorting mirror which makes one period seem charming, another dowdy and a third prettily romantic. It is our business to allow for these errors and to discount them when we are moved to praise, to blame, or to ridicule. The relics of the past which we exhibit in these pages may excite derision, nostalgia or even hatred. I think that they are best regarded as objects of wonder, stupendous and improbable as the bones of the gigantic saurians of the Mesozoic epoch; as such they are beyond envy or criticism. No one in his senses longs to be a diplodocus. It is vain to hanker for the girth or the appetites of the iguanodon; but it would be foolish and ignorant to giggle at, or to disparage, these admirable monsters; they, like the Victorians, deserve our sympathy, for if they were doomed to extinction so are we; and we may think ourselves lucky if we have the honour to be fossilized.

D

A NOTE ON THE PHOTOGRAPHS

by

HELMUT GERNSHEIM

PHOTOGRAPHY, so warmly welcomed in 1839, was fiercely attacked when it asserted its independence and became a successful rival of all but front-rank artists. Landseer, when asked "Will photography be of any use to artists?" replied with a bitter pun, " No, it will always be a foe-to-graphic art."

It is a curious fact that whilst most Victorian "High Art" has long been relegated to the cellars of our art galleries, the everyday art of photography, that much despised Victorian offspring, is gradually being rescued from junk shops and rehabilitated. Ten years ago an attempt to illustrate English life during the last hundred years solely by photographs would have been an almost impossible undertaking. Even today our task has not been an easy one, for neither photographic news agencies nor museums have so far had sufficient foresight to visualise the value of early photographs as the most authentic historic and social illustrations. More than one leading Fleet Street photo-agency considering the scope of our book, assured us that it was a hopeless undertaking to search for photographs earlier than about 1890. Luckily I have been collecting Victorian photographs for years, so that the earlier part of the book actually presented less difficulty than the later period.

Our aim was not to illustrate historical events but the life of the people—the pleasures and sorrows of the English. Even then, many themes had necessarily to be omitted in order to keep within the limits of two hundred illustrations.

Apart from limitations of space, we had to contend with the technical limitations inherent in the nature of early photography. The inability of the daguerreotype and calotype processes to record action was very disconcerting. Until 1855 photographers had to confine themselves almost exclusively to three classes of subject: portraits, architectural views, and landscapes—subjects which the new art could represent much more quickly and cheaply than the old arts. To attempt to record moving objects with cumbersome apparatus and slow negative materials was out of the question. For this reason no photographs of the Great Exhibition, 1851 (No. 1) show any people, though when reproduced in illustrated papers—which could only be done by engraved copies —'life' was added by the engraver. Exposures were just short enough to allow the taking of outdoor groups, provided the photographer impressed upon his sitters the necessity of keeping still during the exposure, as in Nos. 12 and 39. Although taken slightly earlier than our period, the four beautiful groups by David Octavius Hill and Robert Adamson have been included because they are eminently suitable illustrations of our theme, and there were no photographs of the early 'fifties which could have taken their place.

A NOTE ON THE PHOTOGRAPHS

The general introduction of the collodion plate and the widespread use of the stereoscopic camera, employing a comparatively small plate, reduced exposures drastically from minutes to seconds. By 1855 it was possible to increase the range of subjects to include street life and domestic scenes, and even the very early news photograph of unusual historical interest shown in No. 11.

Although the great majority of interior scenes such as the ballroom (No. 19) or the wedding (No. 16) had to be staged, their value as social documents is in no way diminished since they are contemporary and made for a critical public which would have scorned anything but a true-to-life picture. Instantaneous photography of such social functions has only become possible during the last twenty-five years.

Our great-grandparents employed their ample leisure in a much more positive way than the average person today. They were always eager to improve their minds and showed tremendous enthusiasm for the Crystal Palace and other exhibitions like the Polytechnic Institution and the Adelaide Gallery, and the many panoramas, dioramas, kaloramas, kineoramas—enormous paintings of distant lands, with changing light effects, which in some measure may be considered the forerunners of travel films. No wonder that the stereoscope found a place in every drawing-room, for it provided "refined amusement combined with useful instruction"—the criterion of Victorian recreation. The stereoscope was regarded as the optical wonder of the age, for the small slides with their double pictures presented an appearance of astonishing reality and solidity when seen in the instrument. In 1855 the London Stereoscopic Company advertised a stock of 10,000 different stereoscopic pictures—famous buildings, places of historic interest, foreign views—and like a modern illustrated magazine, they were always on the alert to add novelties, and sent their staff photographers abroad as far as the Middle East and America. With increasing popularity a lowering of taste set in and the stereoscope became the poor man's picture gallery. 'Comics' (Nos. 20, 31, 33, 34) and even mildly suggestive scenes (No. 32) now appeared; also pictures of social activities of the upper classes, which had the same function as some present-day Hollywood films—to give a glimpse of luxurious living to those furthest removed from it.

Two author-photographers, J. Thomson and Adolphe Smith, produced a most valuable documentation of the life and work of the poorer classes in the mid-seventies (Nos. 55, 57, 58, 60, 62, 69, 70, 71, 72, 73, 75, 76), a kind of sequel to Henry Mayhew's important survey, London Labour and the London Poor, which had appeared twenty-five years previously. Their illustrations provide an important section of this book, for although there exist many photographs of the life of the upper classes, few photographers considered it worth while to portray the harder phases of life.

The popularisation of the dry plate about 1880, and still more the advent of the Kodak roll-film camera and other hand cameras, permitting a large number of exposures to be made in quick succession, allowed much greater freedom of movement to the photographer and made possible a far wider range of subjects. In the 1890's there was a craze for "detective" cameras disguised as parcels, in hats, in cravats, in the handles of walking sticks, and such pictures as the flirtations on Yarmouth beach (No. 109) and the Bloomer girls in No. 114 can really be counted among the forerunners of "candid camera" snapshots.

This was the period when press photography began in earnest. The half-tone block, introduced in English illustrated papers as a novelty in 1883, retained the photographic quality of the picture in the reproduction and allowed it to be printed satisfactorily along with the rapidly-machined letterpress. By the end of the century it had practically superseded the wood-engravings hitherto used. In 1890 the *Daily Graphic*, the first picture daily, was started, and this brought in its train photographic journalism—photographs specially taken for the press. Four years later the first press agency was founded with the express purpose of supplying illustrated papers and journals with photographs. The proprietors made arrangements with photographers in every part of the country and were able to promise to "secure any photograph not in stock within 24 hours, and in particularly important cases, in 6 to 12 hours".

The last important stage in photographic illustration, as far as we are concerned, was the coming of the Leica in 1925, which heralded for better or worse the era of the miniature camera. With it the whole tendency of the progress of photography towards smaller cameras, shorter exposures, and the attainment of a quick succession of snapshots, reached its logical conclusion. The miniature camera has become the recording machine of everyday life in almost everybody's hands, and has given rise to a new kind of press photography—pictures which are not posed but natural and revealing. To obtain unfamiliar shots of familiar subjects (No. 199) or elusive ones (No. 197) is the quest of the illustrated weeklies. But the function of photography is much greater than that. It provides an indispensable commentary on our daily life, and a powerful force in awakening the social conscience. Hutton's unforgettable picture of the unemployed man (No. 146), and the Eton boys (No. 159), are a much more gripping and convincing commentary on the situation than the most elaborate newspaper article. What Gustave Doré accomplished in his dramatic pen drawings of London can today be achieved by a photographer equal in his powers of vision to those of Doré, with the additional advantage that we know the photographer's pictures must be true and in no way tempered by artistic imagination.

PLATES

1. CRYSTAL PALACE INTERIOR, 1851

Half unpacked, the triumphs of an ostentatious epoch lie dwarfed beneath the vast cage of bare, steel girders. Despite gloomy prophecies, the Prince Consort's bold venture succeeded. It was hailed as the starting point of a happier age. Classes would be reconciled and nations pacified.

2. MR AND MISS
CHALMERS,
c. 1845

These three portraits by Octavius Hill provide
an intimate picture of the Victorian family, the
essential unit and social ideal of the nation. The

continued opposite

3. THE GORDON FAMILY,
*c.*1845

4. DR AND MRS CHALMERS,
*c.*1845

charm, the dignity, and the tranquillity of a prosperous middle-class home are well conveyed in the long poses of early photography.

5. THE GEOGRAPHY LESSON, *c*.1851

Children in large quantities were a characteristic of the
Victorian scene. Here a gentleman, presumably Papa,
instructs his family in the use of the globe. The youngest
child is furnished with a handsome picture book, containing a fine engraving of the Maison Carrée.

6. RECREATION AT HOME, *c.*1856

A passion for decorating every available surface persisted throughout the century. Prodigious energy was expended on making a room genteel. Note the table-cloths and the glass cases, the lamp and the wall-paper. The gentleman in the foreground is looking at photographs through a stereo-scope, while his daughters play billiards.

7. LEWIS CARROLL'S AUNTS PLAYING CHESS, *c.*1858

8. HARROD'S SHOP, 1849 (A modern reconstruction)

A shop was still a place where goods were held in bulk to be divided, mixed and weighed out for the customer. A few branded products will be recognised, but the modern display of graded, blended, tinned, cartoned, labelled, portioned, and pre-digested products was unknown. The sugar is in loaves, to be split into lumps. There are moulds and a pat for butter. Also a pestle and mortar, twists of paper instead of bags, bundles of firewood, and scales in constant use.

9. PLOUGHMAN IN
EAST ANGLIA, 1887

10. AGRICULTURAL
MACHINERY AT
THE GREAT EX-
HIBITION, 1851

The development of the countryside was more uneven than that of the towns. The wooden plough was old-fashioned in 1851, but it persisted in remote places until our own times. Until the motor engine came into the fields, modernity could hardly go further than the traction engine, the threshing drum, and the seed drill. Behind them rises Marochetti's statue of Richard Cœur de Lion, now outside the Houses of Parliament. The old, the new, and the archaistic all had their places in nineteenth-century England.

11. VISIT OF QUEEN VICTORIA AND PRINCE ALBERT WITH NAPOLEON III AND THE EMPRESS EUGENIE TO THE CRYSTAL PALACE, SYDENHAM, 1855

The Crystal Palace was too august a monument to be forgotten (it will reappear later in this book). Too inconvenient to be kept in Hyde Park, it was translated to Sydenham. There it was visited by the Emperor and Empress of the French, our Allies against Russia. The pacific hopes of 1851 had already come to grief.

12. RE-ERECTION OF THE CRYSTAL PALACE AT SYDENHAM, 1853

**13. CRIMEAN WAR. A QUIET
DAY AT THE MORTAR-BATTERY,
1855**

These two war pictures convey a notion
of the squalor and tedium of the long
seige of Sebastopol. The officer seated
in a wheelbarrow displays more dignity
and less abandon than the navvy in the
opposite picture.

**14. CRIMEAN WAR.
CAMP LIFE, 1855**

15. PROPOSAL, *c.*1857

Match-making varied between the dangerous liberties of America and the businesslike arrangements of the Continent. Above we have the elements of the process. A proposal is made by a Crimean hero. He flings his helmet upon a chair and, disdaining the aid of two hassocks, kneels upon the carpet to demand the heart and hand of a young person who appears fresh from the nursery. The marriage ceremony (*right*) is not typical. It is certainly high, perhaps foreign.

16. WEDDING, *c.*1857

The music lesson, like the drawing lesson, is a form of conspicuous consumption and is considered an aid to marriage. The pupils are there to be seen, rather than to be heard. The same may be said of the piano.

Finally, the home, swept, but not without difficulty, for it is abundantly garnished.

18. INTERIOR, *c*.1855

E

This scene of decorous jollity requires little comment; but notice the utter gloom of the gentleman sitting out with a chaperone.

Table-turning was a new sport in the 'fifties. Those who conjured spirits for money were soon ready to produce photographs of phenomena which could not be seen in daylight. This scene, however, is an open pleasantry.

20. THE GHOST, *c*.1857

21. WARMWELL HOUSE, 1863

22. AMATEUR ORCHESTRA AT
EGERTON HOUSE, c.1860

23. **PARTIE DE CAMPAGNE,** *c.*1859

Consider the structural problems encountered by a crinoline
during a violent flirtation on a grassy bank. As Mr James Laver
puts it, "The crinoline was in a constant state of agitation".

24. MARGATE BEACH, *c.*1858

The gentle breezes of Margate might serve to discompose the picture, but even the top-hat seems to be certain of its security. The strange thing about Victorian beach scenes is that sand and sea play remarkably little part. Even the bathing machines in the background appear untidily rejected, and the holiday-makers (if they *are* on holiday) seem to have been lifted straight from their drawing-rooms on to the sand.

25. VIEW AT HAREWOOD HOUSE, 1860

Here, stabilised, the wide skirts complete the stately splendour of the scene.
They are perfectly in accord with all the other paraphernalia of the leisure
class. In gardens such as these, looking out upon vast and pleasant estates,
the landed gentry could feel assured of its own dignified solidity.

26. DEER STALKING IN SCOTLAND, 1859

The deer forest was a comparatively new toy of the very rich.
Sir Walter Scott, the Gothic Revival, the railways, and the
Prince Consort had contributed to its success.

27. CHARLES DICKENS, *c.*1863

28. WOMEN IRON-WORKERS
IN WALES, *c.*1865

29. SCHOOL, *c.*1856

The pictures of the life of the poor on these two pages, in the days when Miss Carlotta Leclerq played at the Princess Theatre and ginger beer, though sold at a penny and twopence a bottle, was a luxury for most little boys, might well serve as illustrations to Dickens. But the Welsh iron-workers are rather more heroic than most of his heroines.

30. SLUM CHILDREN, *c.*1862

Probably both these pictures were considered naughty. The triangular situation is not clear; if the elderly gentleman is a husband, or a father, why does he enter the room with his hat? If he is no more than a rival, why should the gentleman with the Dundreary whiskers take cover and the lady cast a veil over his topper?

32. THE TOILET, *c.*1860

Fashions in impropriety vary. Witness this heavy Rembrantesque lady in a shift, with her clumsy boots and decrepit foot-bath.

33. "FULL-UP INSIDE," *c.*1857

Two more crinoline jokes.
They continued unabated for years
and years.

34. DRESSING FOR THE PARTY, *c.*1860

35. MOURNING PRINCE ALBERT, 1862

"The shadow of his loss drew like eclipse,
    Darkening the world. We have lost him. He is gone."   *Tennyson.*

36. "THE SOURCE OF ENGLAND'S GREATNESS," *c.* 1865

The Psalms here exhibited begin with the 119th and end with the 128th. They are full of appropriate quotations. Perhaps the last is best: "Thy wife shall be as a fruitful vine by the side of thine house." It completes the elaborate symbolism.

37. CHURCH BAZAAR, *c.*1862

The nineteenth century was not only devout but strict. It organised piety, it abounded in missions and bazaars. Everywhere good works and sweet charity were regulated by prudent committees of ladies and gentlemen. Financially the Established Church was comfortable, but it appears to have corrected this (*left*) by using uncomfortably if devout furniture.

38. BISHOP OF DURHAM, *c.*1863

39. THE REVEREND JAMES FAIRBAIRN AND NEWHAVEN FISHWIVES, *c.*1845

The Reverend James Fairbairn, D.D., of the Free Church, is perhaps reading his own book *Jonah, His Life and Character* to the fishwives. What British painter of that age could rival the composition of Octavius Hill's photograph?

The *Great Eastern* was one of the rare failures in an age of technical achievements. She was almost impossible to launch. The disappointment killed her creator, the great Brunel. Nevertheless she sailed at last and laid the first Atlantic cable in 1896.

41. THE OPENING OF THE METROPOLITAN RAILWAY, BAKER STREET, 1862

Gladstone is seated in the near truck as the Underground runs through smoke-filled tunnels.

42. INTERNATIONAL EXHIBITION, 1862

This collection of ceramics is no doubt a fair sample. The Latin inscription (just legible above the arch in the first picture), "The Earth is the Lord's and the Plenty thereof," seems a little unfortunate.

43. GROUP OF COMMISSIONERS OF 1862 INTERNATIONAL EXHIBITION

F

45. GRANDMOTHER AND CHILD, c.1863

44. CHILD, c.1865

Some explanation of the ridiculous clothes worn by these children is attempted in the preface to this book.

46. DR. MARY WALKER, c.1864

47. LADY BUTLER, c.1865

The emancipated, or would-be emancipated, woman was a sign of the times. She grew ever more importunate and important. These contrasting pictures reveal how bold was the innovation of the bloomer, although the wearer looks mild enough to us.

48. COACHING, *c.*1871

49. ARCHERY, *c.*1868

50. CROQUET, c.1865

"Some folk," wrote Rudyard Kipling in 1889, "may remember the years before lawn tennis was born when we all played croquet. There were seasons before that, if you will believe me, when even croquet had not been invented, and archery—which was revived in England in 1844—was as great a pest as lawn tennis is now."

51. AMATEUR THEATRICALS AT A COUNTRY HOUSE, c.1865

The photographer called this little group "amateur theatricals." But what play ever involved so curious a collection of period costumes? A *bal masqué* seems more probable. Note how the flavour of the 'sixties pervades the whole.

79

52. CRYSTAL PALACE, 1859

Never did so much greenery flourish indoors. Paxton was originally a gardener and the greenhouse style informs the Crystal Palace. Thousands of conservatories (such as the one shown at the foot of the opposite page) were thrown out from the drawing-rooms of town dwellings. They were supposed to promote not only vegetable growth, but sentimental passions.

This photograph illustrates the contemporary joke:

Lady: Your character is satisfactory, but I am particular about one thing: I wish my servants to have plenty, but I don't allow any waste.

Buttons: Oh no, 'm. I'd eat and drink till I busted, 'm, rather than waste anything, 'm.

54. CONSERVATORY, *c.* 1870

55. ITALIAN STREET MUSICIANS, 1876

56. CROSSING SWEEPER, c.1860

82

57. PUBLIC DISINFECTORS, 1876

London spread, vicious, grimy and aimless, into the Home Counties. It had its pleasures. Here are two of the more reputable, the "pub" and street music made by small Italian boys exploited by the padrone of Saffron Hill. English boys made a precarious living out of the city's filth. The first signs of reform are represented by the public disinfectors. They bear a box containing a portable oven. They look depressed, as well they may.

58. PUBLIC HOUSE, 1876

60. SHOE-SHINE, 1876

59. "HAVE A TUNE, MISS?" c.1860

62. HANSOM CAB, 1876

61. "SIX TIMES FOR A HA'PENNY," c.1860

85

64. TICHBORNE CLAIMANT, 1867

The bounce of the Victorian scoundrel, Orton "the Claimant", was such that he persuaded Lady Tichborne to believe that he was her long lost son and heir,

63. JOHN RUSKIN AND DANTE GABRIEL ROSSETTI, 1863

Ruskin, grand arbiter of taste, champion of Turner, the pre-Raphaelites and Miss Rose la Touche, supports himself as best he may upon the gifted but unsteady arm of Rossetti,

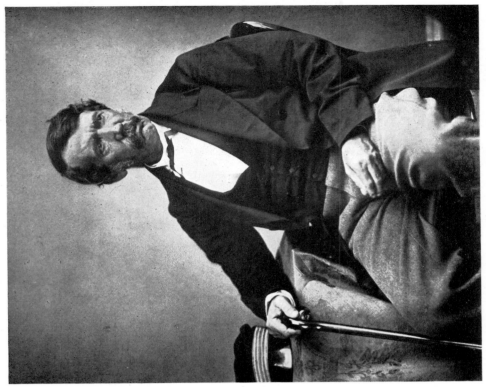

66. DAVID LIVINGSTONE, 1864

Livingstone, the Victorian hero, explorer, big-game hunter, model of courage and tenacity and, above all things, a Christian and a missionary.

65. MRS WILLIAM MORRIS (JANE BURDEN), c.1864

The dress, the hair-style, the attitude, the features of Jane Burden reappear distorted and sentimentalised in the drawings of Rossetti.

67. VICTORIAN FERTILITY, c.1868

68. MUTUAL DEVOTION, *c.*1872

69. STREET PHOTOGRAPHER, 1876

70. OMNIBUS, 1876

71. RECRUITING SERGEANTS, 1876

The "Mitre and Dove" was a recruiting centre where poor gulls accepted a pint and the Queen's shilling. Then, having drilled beyond endurance, they were sent to fight on the frontiers of an Empire which, for sixty years, was never involved in a major war, but never entirely at peace.

72. OLD CLOTHES SHOP, 1876

One of the most brilliant photographs in this book brings to life the hanks of dirty cloth with which everyone, rich and poor, clothed their voluminous forms.

G

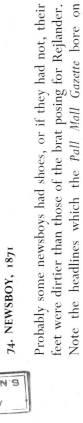

74. NEWSBOY, 1871

Probably some newsboys had shoes, or if they had not, their feet were dirtier than those of the brat posing for Rejlander. Note the headlines which the *Pall Mall Gazette* bore on October 21st, 1871.

73. POOR WOMAN WITH BABY, 1876

A baby-sitter. The mother works from ten till four, and again from eight till ten. The care of the child costs the price of a cup of tea and a slice of bread.

75. STREET DOCTOR, 1876

These quacks had a jargon of their own—"Crocus Latin." "Our profession," said one of them, "is known as 'crocussing', and our decoctions as 'fakes' or 'rackets'."

76. ITALIAN ICE-CREAM MAN, 1876

The ices were sold at a halfpenny each by Neapolitans or Calabrians. In the year when this photograph was taken there were 309 deaths from typhoid in England and Wales.

The evictions shown (*left*) followed the collapse of the trade union led by Joseph Arch. Speaking of muzzle-loaders, Jeffries says: "Most men who have had much to do with guns have burst one or more." The breechloader therefore came as a blessing in the 'sixties. But progress could take other forms.

78. SNIPE SHOOTING ON THE NORFOLK BROADS, 1885

79. THE BARLEY HARVEST, 1887

80. REED HARVEST ON
THE NORFOLK
BROADS, 1885

95

81. "THREE MEN IN A BOAT," *c.*1885

Jerome K. Jerome's novel was being written when the above
picture was taken. The eighteenth century had discovered
Nature, the nineteenth found the countryside, also the moral
virtues of manly exercise.

82. RIDING IN THE PARK, 1883

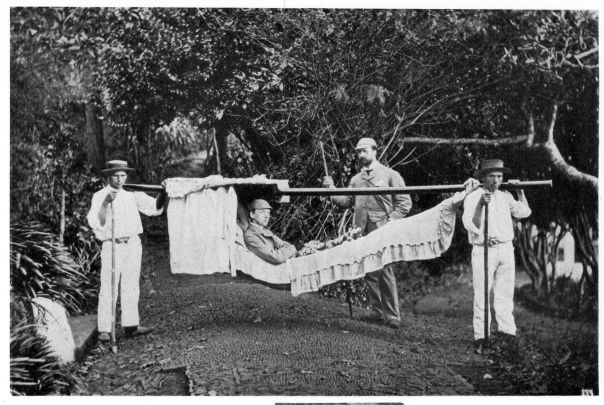

83. PLEASURES OF TRAVEL IN MEXICO, c.1886

Naturally lazy people were sometimes
bullied into going for walks; some
could plead the privilege of their sex;
others shamelessly insisted on being
transported.

84. TRICYCLING, c.1884

97

85. WILLIAM MORRIS, 1889

86. DISRAELI, 1873

87. GLADSTONE
ELECTIONEERING, 1885

"So like a shattered column lay the king." He looks as though he might easily be sick. They are going to lose an oar. Something unexpected has happened to the moon, and to the water. In fact Mrs Cameron has more poetry than she can deal with. This *tableau vivant* below derives from Lord Leighton, or more probably, from the paintings of Albert Joseph Moore.

89. TABLEAU VIVANT
AT OSBORNE, 1888

Who to-day remembers Val Prinsep, painter of "Miriam Watching Over Moses" and "A Venetian Lover"? Like Mrs Cameron, his aunt, he came under the influence of the Pre-Raphaelites. This is what a moderately successful artist's studio looked like in the year 1880.

91. DOMESTIC INTERIOR, 1889

92. THE PROMENADE
    AT EASTBOURNE,
    c.1885

93. " PENNY-FARTHING " BICYCLES, *c*.1887

94. RESTING AFTER TENNIS, *c.*1876

95. TOURISTS CROSSING GLACIER, *c.*1885

97. ELLEN TERRY AND HENRY IRVING IN "OLIVIA," 1885

96. MRS. CORNWALLIS WEST, c. 1880

Sir Max Beerbohm, in his scholarly monograph on the year 1880, says that there was an effort to raise "the average of aristocratic loveliness—an effort that, but a few years before, would have been surely scouted as quite undignified."

99. LADY RANDOLPH CHURCHILL, 1893

98. OSCAR WILDE, 1891

"Beauty," according to Sir Max, "had existed long before 1880," but "it was Mr Oscar Wilde who managed her *début*." This resulted in "the incursion of American ladies into London. Then it was that these pretty creatures drawled their ways through our greater portals."

101. STREET POSTERS, c.1899

100. CAN-CAN, 1890

Gentlemen of a certain age may derive nostalgic pleasure from this hoarding. For us Dan Leno, Letty Lind, Martin Harvey, Edna May (in *The Belle of New York*), and the late Maxine Elliot are but names. The lady on the left may be Lottie Collins: the attitude is characteristically hers.

102. TRAFFIC OUTSIDE THE GAIETY THEATRE, STRAND, c. 1890

H

103. INTERIOR, c.1894

104. EXHIBITION AT THE PHOTOGRAPHIC SOCIETY, 1891

105. THE PRINCESS OF WALES, _c_.1889

106. LADIES BATHING AT YARMOUTH, 1892

107. A SLADE SCHOOL PICNIC, 1899

The man on the second horse is Orpen. Augustus John sits by him. Albert Rutherston has one foot on the shafts.

110. W. G. GRACE AND
W. L. MURDOCH,
c. 1900

"The Champion" is
easily recognised.
Murdoch, sometime
Captain of the Aus-
tralians, wears a cap
and a moustache.

111. EISTEDDFOD, *c.* 1900

112. LADIES' HOCKEY, c.1900

113. CAMBRIDGE PROTESTS AGAINST ADMISSION OF WOMEN
    TO MEMBERSHIP OF THE UNIVERSITY, c.1894

114. BLOOMER GIRLS ON THE QUAY AT BOULOGNE, 1897

115. ROTTEN ROW, c.1900

116. THE GREAT WHEEL AT EARL'S COURT, 1901

The audacious rationals (*opposite, above*), the still undiminished splendours of a horse-drawn epoch and the great ugly iron wheel rising above the dingy roofs of Shepherds Bush, make a fitting conclusion to the display of half a century.

117. BOER WAR NURSES, 1900

118. RELIEF OF MAFEKING, MAY 18th, 1900

The new century began with disasters in South Africa. Casualties were light, but the reverses were humiliating. The defence and relief of Mafeking was a creditable feat of arms, but the rejoicings were disproportionate. Said a foreign observer: "On dirait que l'Angleterre avait conquis l'Europe."

119. CHILDREN AT ONE OF THE
    FIRST CRÈCHES, 1904

These pictures are made for the anthro-
pologist. Observe the circle of children,
their sun-hats, the wheels and the vegetable
symbol round which they girate. Add to
this the taut convexities of Miss Clifford.
Solar worship, sympathetic magic and
matriarchal cults may be freely deduced.

120. CAMILLE CLIFFORD, 1906

121. AN EARLY CINEMA ON AN ENGLISH FAIRGROUND, *c.*1905

122. HOLBORN TELEPHONE EXCHANGE, *c.*1903

123. OPENING OF KINGSWAY BY EDWARD VII, 1905

Royalty was still horse-drawn, but new techniques were on their way. They had been on their way for some time. In April, 1881, *Punch* greeted the new age:

> "Here's the telephone taking the words that we say,
> And the telegraph's marvellous flight;
> There's the light that's electric turns darkness to day
> And the photophone* sounds through the night.
> While the phonograph keeps for historical page
> All the tales of the wonders of Edison's age."

*The photophone was what we call a sound-track.

124. FIRST RACE MEETING OF BROOKLANDS AUTOMOBILE RACING CLUB, JULY 6TH, 1907

125. MOTOR CAR, 1907

The advent of the internal combustion engine changed a great many things, the appearance of street and sky, the lives of millions of people. The Cadillac Model M (*opposite, below*) was a portent in its day. No less interesting is the cottage architecture of the bonnet of the third car at Brooklands.

126. FIRST U.K. AERIAL POST, 1911

127. AIRBORNE, 1908

128. BALLOON
RACE FROM
RANELAGH,
1906

129. HENLEY
REGATTA,
1912

130. OLYMPIC GAMES, 1908

The English did badly in the Olympic Games. This was still a source of wonder. The Italian Dorando (seen here) was first in the Marathon, collapsed at the tape, was held up by his friends, disqualified and consoled with a special medal. (*Below*) Ascot mourning for Edward VII

131. BLACK ASCOT, 1910

132. SOCIAL STRATA AT THE RACES, 1907

Class divisions remained pre-
cise. The difference between
the top hats and the cloth caps
is, literally, one of rank. The
straw hats on the fringes of
society get the worst of both
worlds.

**133. SUFFRAGETTES
ELECTIONEERING, 1908**

The reasonable ladies with their strange and much placarded vehicle (*opposite*, *below*) are less remembered than the militants. Emily Davies flung herself beneath the King's horse crying "Votes for Women!", and died a martyr.

135. CAPTAIN SCOTT'S SHIP "TERRA NOVA,"
AT THE ICE-FOOT, 1911

Peary found the North Pole in 1908. Amundsen, outstripping Scott by about a month, reached the South Pole on December 14th, 1912. The exploration of the Earth was at an end.

136. MR. CHURCHILL AT THE SYDNEY STREET SIEGE, 1911

137. THE "TITANIC" LEAVING BELFAST ON HER ILL-FATED MAIDEN VOYAGE, 1912

138. "WAR OF MOVE-MENT," 1914-18

The country went to war with enthusiasm and at once began to look for an army. Civilians were easily enticed into khaki. Horses had more sense. Wooden mounts were therefore provided to train heroes to charge across Germany.

139. WAR RECRUITING AT WALHAM GREEN, 1914

140. STRETCHER-BEARERS IN BELGIUM, AUGUST, 1917

141. WOMEN MUNITION
WORKERS, 1914-18

In this manner the battle for emancipation was won. Militancy triumphed at last under the Union Jack.

142. ARMISTICE DAY IN TRAFALGAR SQUARE, 1918

The end came with starvation and revolution in Central Europe. The crowds rejoiced, supposing that Germany would be severely punished; supposing, also, that President Wilson's fourteen points would set the world to rights. The fact that these aims were incompatible brought everything to grief. The true victors were perhaps in Moscow: but the Bolsheviks were in no mood for rejoicing on November 11th, 1918.

129

143. PAVLOVA AT COVENT GARDEN, 1928

144. DAME MELBA BROADCASTING FROM THE MARCONI STATION AT CHELMSFORD, 1920

The old world of entertainment, though still very much alive (ballet prospered exceedingly after the war), discovered strange rivals. 2 L.O. began to address the world from Savoy Hill, and here we have Dame Nellie Melba with a microphone worthy of herself.

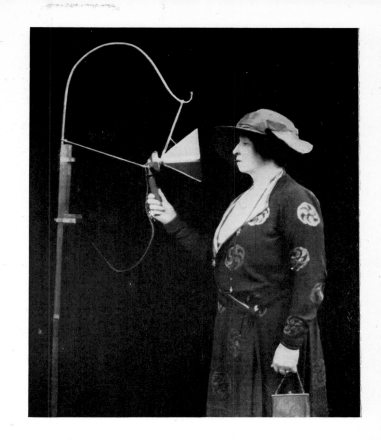

145. RUDOLPH VALENTINO IN "THE EAGLE", c.1924

There must be thousands who remember the time when they worshipped Valentino's shadow. Some may even be able to say just what he and Miss Vilma Banky were about to do at this critical juncture of "The Eagle". There were scenes of wildest despair outside the hospital where he died. Afterwards the faithful swore never to forget. Did they?

146. UNEMPLOYED MAN WITH DOG

There were post-war troubles (some of them familiar). Housing, quarrels between Allies, disillusion about the League, revolt in the Empire, unemployment and strikes, which culminated in the General Strike and defeat of the miners in 1926.

147. EMERGENCY TRANSPORT IN GENERAL STRIKE, 1926

148. SCENE AT THE SERPENTINE, c.1925

149. KING GEORGE V AND QUEEN MARY ON THE MINIATURE RAILWAY AT WEMBLEY, 1924

The high-light of the Wembley Exhibition was a life-size statue of the Prince of Wales in butter. But this homely scene was in its own way, typical.

150. EPSOM RACES, 1928

These shapeless abbreviated sacks once charmed us. All experience shows that future generations will understand why we were charmed. Now we do not.

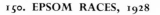
151. AMY JOHNSON, 1930

Alcock and Brown flew the Atlantic in 1919, but public excitement about long - distance flights began with Lindbergh. Thereafter brave young people in search of glory began to fly in all directions. Miss John— son is here seen at the end of a flight from Brisbane.

152. MEET OF FOXHOUNDS AT THEOBALDS PARK, PASSING THROUGH THE TEMPLE BAR, *c.*1932

153. GREYHOUND RACING, *c.*1935

No power in Britain can draw as many people together as a Cup Final or the Derby. Even those who seek to avoid the traffic create new traffic blocks. Sunday evening traffic returning from the country was more dangerous than Oxford Street. (Note how, by 1936, women had lengthened their skirts and rediscovered their waists.)

154. CUP-TIE FEVER, 1946

155. DERBY TRAFFIC, c.1943

156. OXFORD STREET, *c.*1936

157. DERBY CROWD, *c.*1936

158. OPERA-GOER ARRIVING AT COVENT GARDEN, 1937

London shares with Nice the distinction of having its opera house in a vegetable market. This leads to remarkable juxtapositions.

Here the juxtaposition is even more striking.

159. CONTRASTS AT ETON v. HARROW MATCH AT LORD'S, 1937

138

160. THE POTTERIES, 1932

Idle factories and depressed areas were left by the great slump of 1929. Unemployment seemed incurable and there were some who turned to desperate remedies.

161. UNEM-
PLOYEDS'
"COFFIN"
AT No. 10,
1939

K

162. MOSLEY INSPECTS
HIS MEN, 1936

There was plenty of warning this time. Nationalist tyrannies were established over half Europe and the tyrants found imitators here.

163. REFUGEE CHILDREN ARRIVE IN LONDON FROM VIENNA, 1938

London was full of the victims of Fascism. Many were children who had committed the crime of having Jewish parents.

Irresolute, but obstinate, Mr Chamberlain led his country into an impossible attempt at appeasement, until at last it became clear that we had to prepare (*below*) for the consequences of our policy.

164. MR CHAMBERLAIN RETURNS FROM MUNICH, SEPTEMBER 30th, 1938

165. A.R.P. DEMONSTRATION WITH BURNING "BOMBER," 1939

K*

**166. ANXIETY
AMONG THE
STATUES,** 1942

**167. INVASION
SCARE,** 1941

Even now one may see farm carts on which the owner's
address is obliterated lest it give a clue to the invader.
These forlorn signposts were an unnecessary sacrifice. For
years they had perplexed motorists: they might have perplexed Nazis.

For most people the war began with an anti-climax. Windows were papered, evacuees and civil servants were installed, rationing came into force. Hermes and Aphrodite (*opposite*) took cover and Poland was overrun.

168. INTRODUCTION OF
RATIONING, 1940

169. GOVERNMENT OFFICE IN COUNTRY HOUSE DURING 1939-45 WAR

143

170. LAND ARMY GIRLS

171. FACTORY WORKERS, 1939-45

172. A FALLING BUILDING IN THE BLITZ

173. PAVEMENT ARTIST, *c.* 1943

The screever, or pavement artist, deserves a place on his own merits. Here are not only patriotic cartoons, but two traditional motifs—the formal still life and the cottage landscape.

There were two main showers of bombs. A minority took refuge from the night bombing (1940-41). From the flying bomb and the rocket there was no escape.

174. RESCUE WORK AFTER A V-2 FELL ON
FARRINGDON MARKET, 1944

175. UNDERGROUND SHELTER, ALDWYCH STATION, 1940

176. TANK FOR RUSSIA, 1941

Sights such as this were common, especially after the battle of Stalingrad. There had not been such enthusiasm for an ally since Frederick, King of Prussia, defeated our enemies at Rossbach.

177. "RAINBOW CORNER," SHAFTESBURY AVENUE, 1944

Our other ally was much more familiar. He was, indeed, ubiquitous, and we came to know his faults and his virtues.

Such scenes as these were common at a time when Londoners had lost count of the number of exiled governments quartered upon them.

179. V.E. DAY IN FLEET STREET, 1945

The end of the war came, not with a whimper but with a fearful bang. When the radio-active dust had settled, there was a shocked silence. 1945 had fewer illusions than 1918.

180. SQUATTERS AT ABBEY LODGE, ST. JOHN'S WOOD, 1946

The new Government had plenty of headaches. For the man in the street the worst was that he remained in the street, having no home of his own.

181. TEMPORARY HOUSES, c.1947

183. LONGLEAT ON SHOW, 1949

England's social revolution continued on
its courteous way. No frenzied Jacquerie
but high death duties opened the gates of
great houses.

We had become less strict and less intolerant. The display of limbs (*below*)
would not have been conceivable fifty
years earlier. One might suppose that
the climate had changed. A glance at the
other photograph will dispel that illusion.

184. R.A.F. JET ENGINES CLEARING
HUGE SNOWDRIFTS FROM
RAILWAYS, FEBRUARY, 1947

185. THE SERPENTINE. HEAT WAVE, JULY, 1949

186. NEW LOOK, APRIL, 1948

The "New Look", as it was once called, is typical of an age which travels by air and plays, not without considerable affectation, at being "Victorian". Such modish extravagances as are shown in the picture *opposite* are in fact less typical of what was actually worn than the dresses in the air-liner and "tavern-car" *below*. In the decoration of the latter piece of rolling-stock we had archaism at its worst.

187. MODERN AIR-LINE COMFORT

188. TAVERN-CAR ON BRITISH RAILWAYS, 1949

189. CAFETERIA, 1949

Materially the cafeteria was a possibility in 1850, but we have only to consider the moral difficulties which would have stood between a girl and her lunch to perceive the social change of which she is a symptom.

190. SIDNEY STANLEY'S COCKTAIL PARTY, 1948

Following tremendous rumours of corruption in high places, a public enquiry was held into the affairs of Mr Stanley. The revelations were dramatic enough to displace a minister and to amaze and divert the public. The case ended with a grand entertainment for the press, which had every reason to be grateful to Mr Stanley.

191. HYDE PARK ORATORS, *c.*1947

192. THE BRAINS TRUST, 1948

The speakers in the Park remain a curiosity and a monument to liberty. The speakers on the radio are (*from left to right*) Robert Boothby, C. E. M. Joad, Gilbert Harding (Question Master), and Dr J. Bronowski.

193. TELEVISION, " LES SYLPHIDES," 1946

194. THEATRE QUEUE, 1946

195. GEORGE BERNARD SHAW, 1949

Shaw spanned two centuries. He landed on our shores in the year 1879 and set to work to alter our views on Art, Music, Shakespeare, Ibsen, Wagner, Socialism, Prostitution, Evolution, Carnivorous Diet, Vaccination, and Bernard Shaw. This he did with such complete success that, by 1914, he was a back number. For the next thirty-six years he remained as brilliant a public nuisance as any in our history, and died a grand old man.

196. QUEUE FOR VAN GOGH EXHIBITION AT THE TATE GALLERY, 1948

In an age of queues it is only fair to notice that one of the longest led to a collection of works of art. Forty years ago these same pictures were laughed at by the general public and by most of the critics.

197. SELLING NYLON STOCKINGS, 1949

We had fewer black markets than most of the
countries which suffered shortages. Nylons were
one exception.

198. DELIVERY OF FOOTBALL POOL COUPONS,
  *c.*1949

The promoters of football pools, on the other hand,
remained strictly within the law. They noticed that
a sucker was born every minute, and made the most
of that important fact.

199. AT THE FAIR,
SOUTHEND

Our climate, like our character, is a mass of contradictions. We do not always take our pleasures as sadly as those who doggedly endure the rigours of an English July.

200. MARGATE BEACH, JULY, 1947

201. THE NEW TOWN OF STEVENAGE, 1951

SOURCES

SOURCES

1. Crystal Palace interior, 1851. (Gernsheim collection.)
2. Mr and Miss Chalmers, c.1845. By David Octavius Hill and Robert Adamson. (Gernsheim collection.)
3. The Gordon family, c.1845. By David Octavius Hill and Robert Adamson. (Gernsheim collection.)
4. Dr and Mrs Chalmers, c.1845. By David Octavius Hill and Robert Adamson. (Gernsheim collection.)
5. The geography lesson, c.1851. By A. Claudet. (Gernsheim collection).
6. Recreation at home, c.1856. (Gernsheim collection.)
7. Lewis Carroll's aunts playing chess, c.1858. (Gernsheim collection.)
8. Harrod's shop, 1849 (a modern reconstruction). By Sydney W. Newbery. (Copyright: *The Architectural Review*.)
9. Ploughman in East Anglia, 1887. By P. H. Emerson. (Gernsheim collection.)
10. Agricultural machinery at Great Exhibition, 1851. (Gernsheim collection.)
11. Visit of Queen Victoria and Prince Albert with Napoleon III and Empress Eugenie to the Crystal Palace, Sydenham, April 20th, 1855. (By courtesy of E. J. Denney, Esq.)
12. Re-erection of the Crystal Palace at Sydenham, 1853. By Philip H. Delamotte. (*Picture Post* Library.)
13. Crimean War. A quiet day at the mortar battery, 1855. By Roger Fenton. (Gernsheim collection.)
14. Crimean War. Camp life, 1855. By Roger Fenton. (Gernsheim collection.)
15. Proposal, c.1857. (Gernsheim collection.)
16. Wedding, c.1857. (Gernsheim collection.)
17. Music lesson, c.1856. (Gernsheim collection.)
18. Interior, c.1855. (Gernsheim collection.)
19. At the ball, c.1854. (Gernsheim collection.)
20. The Ghost, c.1857. (Gernsheim collection.)
21. Warmwell House, 1863. (Gernsheim collection.)
22. Amateur orchestra at Egerton House, c.1860. (Gernsheim collection.)
23. Partie de Campagne, c.1859. (Gernsheim collection.)
24. Margate beach, c.1858. (Gernsheim collection.)
25. View at Harewood House, 1860. By Roger Fenton. (Gernsheim collection.)
26. Deer-stalking in Scotland, 1859. (Gernsheim collection.)
27. Charles Dickens, c.1863. (Gernsheim collection.)
28. Women ironworkers in Wales, c.1865. (Gallery of English Costume, Manchester.)
29. School, c.1856. (*Picture Post* Library.)
30. Slum children, c.1862. (*Picture Post* Library.)
31. An awkward moment, c.1856. (Gernsheim collection.)
32. The toilet, c.1860. (Gernsheim collection.)
33. Full up inside, c.1857. (*Picture Post* Library.)
34. Dressing for the party, c.1860. (*Picture Post* Library.)
35. Mourning Prince Albert, 1862. By Bambridge. (Gernsheim collection.)
36. "The Source of England's Greatness", c.1865. (Gernsheim collection.)
37. Church bazaar, c.1862. (Gernsheim collection.)
38. Bishop of Durham, c.1863. (Gernsheim collection.)
39. The Rev. James Fairbairn and Newhaven fishwives, c. 1845. By David Octavius Hill and Robert Adamson. (Gernsheim collection.)
40. The "Great Eastern" steamship, 1858. (Gernsheim collection.)
41. Opening of Metropolitan Railway, Baker Street, 1862. (*Picture Post* Library.)
42. International Exhibition, 1862. (Gernsheim collection.)
43. Group of Commissioners of 1862 International Exhibition. (Gernsheim collection.)
44. Child, c.1865. (Gernsheim collection.)
45. Grandmother and child, c.1863. (Gernsheim collection.)
46. Dr Mary Walker, c.1864. (Gernsheim collection.)
47. Lady Butler, c.1865. (Gernsheim collection.)
48. Coaching, c.1871. (Gernsheim collection.)
49. Archery, c.1868. (*Picture Post* Library.)
50. Croquet, c.1865. (Hector Bolitho, Esq.)
51. Amateur theatricals at country house, c.1865. (Gernsheim collection.)
52. Crystal Palace, c.1859. By P. H. Delamotte. (Gernsheim collection.)
53. Lady and page, c.1869. (Gernsheim collection.)
54. Conservatory, c.1870. (Gernsheim collection.)
55. Italian street musicians, 1876. By "J. T. and A. S." (Gernsheim collection.)
56. Crossing sweeper, c.1860. By O. G. Rejlander. (Gernsheim collection.)
57. Public disinfectors, 1876. By "J. T. and A. S." (Gernsheim collection.)
58. Public house, 1876. By "J. T. and A. S." (Gernsheim collection.)
59. "Have a tune, Miss?" c.1860. By O. G. Rejlander. (Gernsheim collection.)
60. Shoe-shine, 1876. By "J. T. and A. S." (Gernsheim collection.)
61. "Six times for a ha'penny", c.1860. By O. G. Rejlander. (Gernsheim collection.)

62. Hansom cab, 1876. By "J. T. and A. S." (Gernsheim collection.)
63. John Ruskin and Dante Gabriel Rossetti, 1863. By W. & D. Downey. (Gernsheim collection.)
64. Tichborne claimant, 1867. (*Picture Post* Library.)
65. Mrs William Morris (Jane Burden), c.1865. (Gernsheim collection.)
66. David Livingstone, 1864. By Thomas Annan. (Gernsheim collection.)
67. Victorian fertility, c.1868. (Gernsheim collection.)
68. Mutual devotion, c.1872. (Gernsheim collection.)
69. Street photographer, 1876. By "J. T. and A. S." (Gernsheim collection.)
70. Omnibus, 1876. By "J. T. and A. S." (Gernsheim collection.)
71. Recruiting sergeants, 1876. By "J. T. and A. S." (Gernsheim collection.)
72. Old clothes shop, 1876. By "J. T. and A. S." (Gernsheim collection.)
73. Poor woman with baby, 1876. By "J. T. and A. S." (Gernsheim collection.)
74. Newsboy, 1871. By O. G. Rejlander. (A. S. Boyer, Esq.)
75. Street doctor, 1876. By "J. T. and A. S." (Gernsheim collection.)
76. Italian ice cream man, 1876. By "J. T. and A. S." (Gernsheim collection.)
77. Eviction of agricultural workers, 1874. (Porcupine Press.)
78. Snipe shooting on the Norfolk Broads, 1885. By P. H. Emerson. (Gernsheim collection.)
79. The barley harvest, 1887. By P. H. Emerson. (Gernsheim collection.)
80. Reed harvest on the Norfolk Broads, 1885. By P. H. Emerson. (Gernsheim collection.)
81. "Three men in a boat" c.1885. By William Taunt. (Gernsheim collection.)
82. Riding in the park, 1883. (Gernsheim collection.)
83. Pleasures of travel in Mexico, c.1880. (Gernsheim collection.)
84. Tricycling, c.1884. (Gernsheim collection.)
85. William Morris, 1889. By Sir Emery Walker. (Gernsheim collection.)
86. Disraeli, 1873. By W. & D. Downey. (Gernsheim collection.)
87. W. E. Gladstone electioneering, 1885. By J. Birtles, Warrington. (Gernsheim collection.)
88. "The Passing of Arthur" by Julia Margaret Cameron, 1874. (Gernsheim collection.)
89. Tableau vivant at Osborne, 1888. By Hughes and Mullins. (Gernsheim collection.)
90. Val Prinsep, c.1880. By J. P. Mayall. (Gernsheim collection.)
91. Domestic interior, 1889. By Robert Slingsby. (Gernsheim collection.)
92. The promenade at Eastbourne, c.1885. By G. S. R. Lavis. (Gernsheim collection.)
93. "Penny-farthing" bicycles, c.1887. (*Picture Post* Library.)
94. Resting after tennis, c.1876. (Gernsheim collection.)
95. Tourists crossing glacier, c.1885. (Gernsheim collection.)
96. Mrs Cornwallis West, c.1880. (Gernsheim collection).
97. Ellen Terry and Henry Irving in *Olivia*, 1885. (*Picture Post* Library.)
98. Oscar Wilde, 1891. (Gernsheim collection.)
99. Lady Randolph Churchill, 1893. (Gernsheim collection.)
100. Can-can, 1890. (*Picture Post* Library.)
101. Street posters, c.1899. (Aerofilms.)
102. Traffic outside the Gaiety Theatre, Strand, c.1890. (*Picture Post* Library.)
103. Interior, c.1894. (Gernsheim collection.)
104. Exhibition at Photographic Society, 1891. (Gernsheim collection.)
105. Princess of Wales, c.1889. By Alice Hughes. (Gernsheim collection.)
106. Ladies bathing at Yarmouth, 1892. By Paul Martin. (Leonard Russell, Esq.)
107. A Slade School picnic, 1899.
108. Throwing off reserve, 1893. By Paul Martin. (Leonard Russell, Esq.)
109. Flirtations on Yarmouth beach, 1892. By Paul Martin. (*Picture Post* Library.)
110. W. G. Grace and W. L. Murdoch, c.1900. (*Picture Post* Library.)
111. Eistedfodd, c.1900. (Gernsheim collection.)
112. Ladies' hockey, c.1900. (Gernsheim collection.)
113. Cambridge protests against admission of women to membership of the University, c.1894. (By courtesy of Stearn & Sons, Cambridge.)
114. Bloomer girls on the quay at Boulogne, 1897. By Paul Martin. (Leonard Russell, Esq.)
115. Rotten Row, c.1900. (*Picture Post* Library.)
116. The Great Wheel at Earl's Court, 1901. (Gernsheim collection.)
117. Boer War nurses, 1900. By Horace W. Nicholls.
118. Relief of Mafeking, May 18th, 1900. (Sport & General.)
119. Children at one of the first creches, 1904. (Clark & Hyde.)
120. Camille Clifford, 1906. (*Picture Post* Library.)
121. "Electric theatre" on an English fairground, c.1905. (Keystone Press Agency.)
122. Holborn telephone exchange, c.1903. (By courtesy of the Postmaster General.)
123. Opening of Kingsway by Edward VII, 1905. (By courtesy of the L.C.C.)
124. First race meeting of Brooklands Automobile Racing Club, July 6th, 1907. (Sport & General.)
125. Motor car, 1907. (*Picture Post* Library.)
126. First U.K. Aerial Post, 1911. (Gernsheim collection.)
127. Airborne, 1908. (*Picture Post* Library.)
128. Balloon race from Ranelagh, 1906. (Topical Press.)

129. Henley Regatta, 1912. (Topical Press.)
130. Olympic Games, 1908. Marathon. (*Picture Post* Library.)
131. Black Ascot, 1910. (Topical Press.)
132. Social strata at the races, 1907. (Topical Press.)
133. Suffragettes electioneering, 1908. (Topical Press.)
134. Suffragette killed at the Derby, 1913. (Graphic Photo Union.)
135. Capt. Scott's ship "Terra Nova" at the ice foot, 1911. By H. G. Ponting. (Paul Popper Photographic Agency.)
136. Mr Churchill at the Sydney Street siege, 1911. (P.A. Reuter.)
137. The *Titanic* leaving Belfast on her ill-fated maiden voyage, 1912. (Topical Press.)
138. "War of movement," 1914-18. (Clark & Hyde.)
139. 1914 War. Recruiting at Walham Green. (Graphic Photo Union.)
140. Stretcher bearers, in Belgium, August 1st, 1917. (Imperial War Museum.)
141. Women munition workers, 1914-18. (Graphic Photo Union.)
142. Armistice Day in Trafalgar Square, 1918. (Graphic Photo Union.)
143. Pavlova at Covent Garden, 1928. (*The Times*.)
144. Dame Melba broadcasting from the Marconi station at Chelmsford, 1920. (By courtesy of Marconi's Wireless Telegraph Co. Ltd.)
145. Rudolph Valentino in "The Eagle", c.1924.
146. Unemployed man with dog, 1939. By K. Hutton. (*Picture Post* Library.)
147. Emergency transport in General Strike, 1926. (Graphic Photo Union.)
148. Scene at the Serpentine, c.1925. (Fox Photos.)
149. King George V and Queen Mary on the miniature railway at Wembley, 1924. (*The Times*.)
150. Epsom races, 1928. (L.N.A.)
151. Amy Johnson, 1930. (*New York Times* Photos.)
152. Meet of foxhounds at Theobalds Park, c.1932. (Fox Photos.)
153. Greyhound racing, c.1935. (P.A. Reuter.)
154. Cup-tie fever, 1946. (Keystone Press Agency.)
155. Derby traffic, c.1943. (*Picture Post* Library.)
156. Oxford Street, c.1936. (C.O.I.)
157. Derby crowd, c.1936. (*The Times*.)
158. Opera-goer arriving at Covent Garden, 1937. (*Daily Herald*.)
159. Contrasts at Eton v. Harrow match at Lords, 1937. (Central Press Photos.)
160. The Potteries, 1932. (*The Times*.)
161. Unemployeds' "coffin" at No. 10, 1939. (Central Press Photos.)
162. Mosley inspects his men, 1936. (Associated Press.)
163. Refugee children arrive in London from Vienna, 1938. (*Planet News*.)
164. Mr Chamberlain returns from Munich, September 30th, 1938. (Fox Photos.)
165. A.R.P. demonstration with burning "bomber", 1939. (Fox Photos.)
166. Anxiety among the statues, 1942. By Helmut Gernsheim. (Gernsheim collection.)
167. Invasion scare, 1941. (Topical Press.)
168. Introduction of Rationing, 1940. (Fox Photos.)
169. Government office in country house during 1939-45 war. (*Illustrated*.)
170. Land Army girls. (Sport & General.)
171. Factory workers, 1939-45. (C.O.I.)
172. A falling building in the blitz. (By courtesy of the Commissioners of City of London Police.)
173. Pavement artist, c.1943. By Douglas Glass. (Black Star.)
174. Rescue work after V.2 fell on Farringdon Market, 1944. (*Picture Post* Library.)
175. Underground shelter, Aldwych station, 1940. (*Planet News*.)
176. Tank for Russia, 1941. (*Daily Herald*.)
177. "Rainbow Corner", Shaftesbury Avenue, 1944. By Albert Creffield. (*New York Times* Photos.)
178. Street dancing in London for France's July 14th, 1943. (*Picture Post* Library.)
179. V.E. Day in Fleet Street. (L.N.A.)
180. Squatters at Abbey Lodge, St. John's Wood, 1946. (Graphic Photo Union.)
181. Temporary houses, c.1947. By Andrey Andersson. (Black Star.)
182. Bomb site playground in Liverpool, 1949. (*Picture Post* Library.)
183. Longleat on show, 1949. (*Picture Post* Library.)
184. R.A.F. jet engines clearing huge snowdrifts from railways. February, 1947. (*Daily Herald*.)
185. The Serpentine. Heat-wave, July, 1949. By Bill Eades. (Black Star.)
186. New Look, April, 1948. (Fox Photos.)
187. Modern airline comfort. (By courtesy of British European Airways.)
188. Tavern car on British Railways, 1949. (By courtesy of British Railways.)
189. Cafeteria, 1949. (*Daily Herald*.)
190. Sidney Stanley's cocktail party, 1948. (*Daily Herald*.)
191. Hyde Park orators, c.1947. (Black Star.)
192. The Brains Trust, 1948. (B.B.C.)
193. Television. "Les Sylphides", 1946. (B.B.C.)
194. Theatre queue, 1946. (*Daily Herald*.)
195. George Bernard Shaw, 1949. By Felix H. Man.
196. Queue for Van Gogh exhibition at the Tate Gallery, 1948. (*New York Times* Photos.)
197. Spiv selling nylon stockings, 1949. By Ronald Haupt.
198. Delivery of football pool coupons, c.1949. (Keystone.)
199. At the fair, Southend, 1938. By K. Hutton. (*Picture Post* Library.)
200. Margate beach, July, 1947. (Keystone.)
201. The New Town of Stevenage, 1949. (Aerofilms Ltd.)